AUTHORS

Alan Murdie LL.B, Barrister is chairman of the Ghost Club (founded in Cambridge in the 19th century) and a member of the Society for Psychical Research. He has personally investigated numerous cases of alleged haunting in Britain and abroad, and has written and broadcast extensively on paranormal topics. The author of ten books, including four on haunted cities in the UK, he also writes monthly column devoted to ghosts for the magazine *Fortean Times.*

Although resident in Bury St. Edmunds since 1966, **Robert Halliday** was born in Cambridge, and has maintained a life-long interest in the city and the surrounding county, having worked for the Churches Conservation Trust in Cambridge. He holds an MA degree in history, has lectured on East Anglian local history and has written articles for popular and academic journals. His previous books include *Around Bury St. Edmunds (In Old Photographs)*; *Suffolk Strange But True* and *Cambridgeshire Strange But True.*

CAMBRIDGE GHOSTS

by

Robert Halliday
&
Alan Murdie

To Dr. Ann Silver
with best wishes and
many thanks from the authors,

Robert Halliday Alan Murdie

Published 2010 by arima publishing

www.arimapublishing.com

ISBN 978 1 84549 453 7

Printed and bound in the United Kingdom

Typeset in Garamond

arima publishing
ASK House, Northgate Avenue
Bury St Edmunds, Suffolk IP32 6BB
t: (+44) 01284 700321
www.arimapublishing.com

CONTENTS

Dedicated to
Cambridge psychical researcher

Tony Cornell

(1923 - 2010)

INTRODUCTION

Cambridge is one of the most haunted cities in Britain, as this selection of reports and stories shows. Ghostly experiences are described by residents, students and visitors alike, and new accounts emerge each year. It is impossible to write about the city without mentioning the university, which has played an important role in the development of Cambridge ghostlore. One reason that so many Cambridge ghosts are known is because some university members have been keen to observe and record paranormal phenomena, starting some of the world's greatest psychic research organisations. Many colleges have resident ghosts as a result of their long histories and the many unusual people who have lived and studied within them. Nor is it co-incidental that university members have used the historic buildings of Cambridge as backdrop for imaginative fictional ghost stories, drawing from their knowledge of arcane and esoteric aspects of college life and academia for inspiration.

However, it must not be forgotten that Cambridge also has a long history as a county town and market centre, and there are many houses, and even open spaces here that have witnessed paranormal phenomena. In 1998 we devised The Cambridge Ghost Walk, which has attracted great interest from all sections of Cambridge society, and many people whom we have met as a result have told us about their experiences, some saying we are the first people in whom they have confided, fearing that they would be ridiculed if speaking openly of having seen a ghost or witnessed psychic activity. We hope this book will demonstrate that such occurrences are far from unusual, and that since some of the finest minds at one of the world's greatest universities have had encounters with the supernatural, these reports from local witnesses deserve serious attention and open-minded consideration.

We have, as far as possible investigated and authenticated all the stories that follow. In the completion of this task we owe a debt to Tony Cornell, one of the most experienced and respected psychic researchers in Cambridge, and the entire United Kingdom, who was a great inspiration and encouragement. The late Dr Hilda Ellis-Davidson of Newnham convened The Cambridge Folklore Group, a sadly missed society and social gathering, which provided innumerable insights in a most convivial setting. The staff of Cambridge's many libraries have been constantly helpful, in particular Chris Jakes and his colleagues at the invaluable Cambridgeshire Collection in Cambridge Central Library; we also thank Suzan Griffiths, the librarian of St. Catherine's College for details about that college and its ghost stories.

We extend further gratitude to Sharon Meijland of the Rainbow Vegetarian Restaurant for her ghost stories (and her hospitality on ghost hunts); Carolina Manosca Grisales for support with photography; Bruce Milner of the Sawston Village History Society for information about and photographs of Sawston Hall and The Tanner's House; Mike Petty M.B.E., founder of the Cambridgeshire Collection and local historian for much information on all things Cambridge; Wendy Reynolds of the Gogmagog Hills for details of ghost stories from that region; Nicholas Rogers of Sidney Sussex College for photographs of Oliver Cromwell's head; Terry Welbourn for information on the work of T. C. Lethbridge; and Daniel Williman for Latin translation.

Three Cambridge University academics proved exceptionally helpful: Dr. Tom Licence of Cambridge University by providing important information on modern ghosts; James Muckle of the University of Nottingham, a Peterhouse graduate, by supplying particulars of the Blue Lady of Peterhouse College; Dr. Ann Silver of Cambridge University in sending crucial facts about the ghosts of Babraham and the Gogmagog Hills.

Local residents who deserve special thanks for telling us about their personal experiences include Cambridge citizens Kathy Skin and the late Philip ('Phil') Butler, together with Bill Clark, the former warden of the Gogmagog Hills, who has provided excellent talks on that locality.

CAMBRIDGE COLLEGE GHOSTS

Cambridge University is famous for its colleges, which give the city centre much of its present character. These large and impressive historic buildings have housed many famous people, and have witnessed many dramatic events, so it is not surprising that some are believed to be haunted.

KING'S COLLEGE

King's College is Cambridge's best known landmark. Commanding a central position in the city, its majestic buildings are recognised internationally, forming the backdrop to countless photographs taken every year. The chapel, built between 1446 and 1547, is one of the glories of medieval architecture, containing the largest display of Renaissance stained glass in its original setting to be seen anywhere in the world. King's College Chapel is also celebrated for its musical tradition, staging a carol service that is broadcast globally every year, to be enjoyed by millions.

King's College Chapel.

The chapel claims some ghost stories. Local folklore quotes such entities as a shadowy phantom that flits along the roof: one legend claims he was a victim of the old student prank of placing objects on the rooftop pinnacles. In Christmas 2003 Alan Murdie met an elderly

Cambridge man whose father was employed at the college in 1900, when he heard horses in the chapel. Was this a ghostly echo of Civil War days when the Roundheads used King's College Chapel as a stable for cavalry horses?

M R James, author of classic ghost stories, in his study at King's College.

King's College should be a place of pilgrimage for all those who enjoy reading ghost stories because of its associations with Montague Rhodes James, better known as M.R. James, who is widely regarded as the author of the finest collection of fictional ghost stories in the English language. The son of the rector of Great Livermere in Suffolk (itself a candidate for the title of 'the most haunted village in England') he entered King's College in 1879, intending to become a clergyman too, but proved such a brilliant student that he was asked to join the college staff. He spent much of his adult life at King's College, as a fellow, tutor, dean, and eventually Provost (or master), while being elected Vice-Chancellor, the university's highest administrative post. He wrote over 200 books and articles about palaeography, medieval art and related subjects including the leading modern version of the apocryphal books of the Bible, in which he displayed a phenomenal grasp of modern and archaic languages. However, it is his collection of thirty fictional ghost stories for which his name endures. He wrote the first of these in 1893, and read it to some college friends. The response was so enthusiastic that he was asked to write more, and every Christmas he would narrate his latest tale by candlelight to an enthralled gathering. Frequently urged to publish, his first volume, *Ghost Stories of an Antiquary* appeared in 1904. Three further selections followed, followed by *Collected Ghost Stories* in 1931. Praise for these was high from the start and they remain perennially popular.

M. R. James replaced the laboured gothic style previously favoured by ghost story writers with realistic and believable contemporary settings, adopting a restrained, antiquarian tone reflecting the scholarly and erudite environment in which he lived. Many of his protagonists are scholars and academics whose dry, bookish lives are progressively disrupted by malevolent and physically dangerous entities. M. R. James stated that he sought to make his fictional ghosts consistent with the spectres of supernatural folklore, and he drew upon a lifetime's research into history, archaeology and esoteric writings to intersperse his writings with invented, but remarkably convincing, extracts from manuscripts, books and folktales. Avoiding 'blood and guts' horror, he created a careful balance between everyday life and an enveloping otherworld, conveying an eerie sense of mystery, which is best brought out when read aloud, and can often become more apparent with repeated reading. Their status as classics is confirmed by the fact they have remained in print for over a century and exert a greater fascination with the passage of time. Scholars speculate that M. R. James experienced several ghostly encounters in his life: certainly he was influenced by dreams and had a particular dislike of spiders.

Classic stories include *Casting The Runes* (adapted as the horror film *Night Of The Demon* in 1957), *The Ash* Tree (set in his home village of Great Livermere), *A Warning To The Curious*, O *Whistle And I'll Come To You My* Lad, and *Lost Hearts.* One of his tales, *The Tractate Middoth*, centres on the old University Library, which, until 1934, was housed in The Old Schools Building, at the corner of Trinity Lane and Senate House Passage, adjacent to King's College. The Tractate Middoth was an ancient Jewish manuscript containing certain supernatural references, and the narrative makes allusions to University life that would have been particularly amusing to members of King's College. Many English ghost story writers would cite M. R. James as one of their great influences: many techniques now used in this genre can be traced to his writings, causing him to be regarded as the originator of the modern ghost story.

King's College: the chapel stands centrally, the Gibbs Building (scene of a macabre tragedy) extends to the right. Clare College, haunted by a Don seeking his lost skeleton, extends to the left (opposite the bridge).

M. R. James vouched for the presence of a ghost at King's College in the large eighteenth century Gibbs Building, which stands southwest of the chapel, facing the River Cam. An eccentric and decidedly morbid academic called Barrett lodged there, keeping a coffin in his rooms. As he grew old Barrett became a worried and frightened man, loosing much of his money and being dogged by bad luck: it was rumoured that dark forces haunted him. One night screams were heard in his lodgings: next morning he was found dead in his coffin, laid there by the spiritual entities with which he communicated during his sinister life. Every year, on the anniversary of his death, Barrett's screams reverberate from his rooms.

MAGDALEN COLLEGE

Magdalen College originated as a hostel for monks studying at the University. Its most famous alumnus was Samuel Pepys, who left his collection of books and manuscripts (including his famous diaries) to the college, where they are housed in the beautiful seventeenth century Pepys Library. The Fellow's Garden of Magdalen College which lies behind the Pepys Library, contains a little-known Cambridge curiosity: a cemetery for the fellows' dogs. It is also the setting for a previously unpublished encounter with the paranormal. Alan Murdie knows a resident member of the academic staff, who, on 19 August 2008, was reading a newspaper in the combination room. It was about 9.15p.m. on an overcast evening, when he was intrigued to hear an owl hooting from a clump of trees near Monk's Walk, a bank between the garden wall and Chesterton Lane. Deciding to investigate he went out to the garden. Crossing the lawn towards the trees, he began to feel uneasy and decided to turn back. As he did so he looked towards the River Cam and saw 'a thinnish male figure, seemingly pale or dressed in white' moving abnormally fast across the ground. At first he thought it might be a cyclist on the other side of the river, but on looking closely he realized it was moving along the Riverside Walk which follows the course of the River Cam. It 'progressed roughly where the path is following its line from the greenhouses towards the end of the garden'. The sense of unease was intensified when he realized it would have had to have passed through a locked gate and was travelling along a gravel path without making any noise. He

Dog's cemetery in the North West corner of the Fellow's Garden at Magdalen College.

Riverside Walk in the Fellow's Garden at Magdalen College.

observed: 'had a runner entered I should have heard the noise, being already in the garden'. The pale figure vanished into the dark trees at the end of the garden. Although feeling uncomfortable, he remained outdoors, looking for the owl and comparing the sight of human figures passing on the opposite bank who looked solid and real, in contrast to the runner who seemed 'weird and unreal'. As soon as he returned indoors he wrote an account of his experience. A member of Magdalen College for nine years, he had been in the Fellow's Garden many times, and never regarded it as an eerie place, or seen anything like the figure before. He later recalled that there had been vague stories of an apparition that haunted the garden, but these were certainly not in his conscious mind at the time. A research student from New Zealand (of Maori descent) has claimed that a particular tree was a focus of spirit activity. The case provides good example of how apparitional experiences occur spontaneously when the witness is not deliberately looking for ghosts or even thinking about them. In his classic book on *Apparitions* (1942) psychic researcher G. N. M. Tyrrell remarked that instead of enquiring 'do you believe in ghosts?', one should ask 'do people experience apparitions?'. The Magdalen College case causes us to conclude that they undoubtedly do.

There is a story that a ghost haunts the Hall and the east end of the north range of the First Court. The bedders do not see it, but say they feel a presence. They call the ghost 'George', but the story is that if it worries them they tell it to 'B∗∗∗∗r Off!' and it goes away.

CORPUS CHRISTI COLLEGE

This statue on the east gable of the Old Master's Lodge at Corpus Christi College is said to be Dr Butts's dog, who kept a faithful watch after his master's suicide.

Corpus Christi College dates from 1352 (the name is Latin for 'the body of Christ'): the fourteenth century Old Court is the oldest college courtyard in Cambridge. The Old Master's Lodge, at the east end of the south range of this court, has been the setting for sinister tragedies. During a plague outbreak in 1632 Dr. Henry Butts, the Master of Corpus, stayed in Cambridge to care for the sick and dying, an experience which affected him deeply, giving him a ghost-like look. But his services were not necessarily appreciated, for when Charles I visited Cambridge Dr. Butts sponsored a play to entertain the king which was a dismal flop, being booed off-stage. Hoping to regain royal favour Dr. Butts suggested that the University sell degrees and give the money raised to the king. When his colleagues rejected this he said 'I perceive that all my actions have been misinterpreted, and therefore I will go home to die'. Ten days later he hanged himself in his Lodge. The east end of the Old Master's Lodge overlooks Freeschool Lane: at the apex of the gable there is a statue of an animal: a Cambridge legend says that this was Dr. Butts's dog, who remained faithful to him until the end, keeping a mournful guard by the dead body.

In the 1820's after Corpus Christi College was enlarged with the construction of the New Court, the upper rooms of the Old Master's

Lodge were converted into student apartments and the lower rooms became kitchens. It has been suggested that when an old building is altered latent psychic energy can be raised and dormant spirits may be roused: this seems to have been the case at the Old Master's Lodge. Strange and inexplicable footsteps and banging noises began to be heard. The catering staff were convinced that a ghost lurked in the kitchens and would not stay there at night. These were tales of frightening apparitions of the upper part of a man or a bodiless head. Walter Moule, a student who became a missionary in China, stayed here and often heard a loud banging like a trapdoor slamming (or maybe the falling of the trap on a gallows). One fateful day his uncle Charles, a senior fellow, was seen crawling out of the room on his hands and knees in stark terror. Extremely frightened (not to mention deeply embarrassed) Charles Moule never revealed what had scared him so dreadfully.

The Old Court of Corpus Christi College; the right hand range contains the college hall; the Old Master's Lodge stands to the left of this, just past the bay window.

In 1903 Llewellyn Powys (who became a prominent author) lodged on the west side of the Old Court. One afternoon he looked through the window to see the head and shoulders of a long-haired man leaning from a dormer window at the top of the Old Lodge. It remained motionless for three minutes. Llewellyn went into another room for a better view, but in that short time the figure disappeared. Llewellyn ran across to the room with the dormer window, but found it locked: the student who lodged there had left for the afternoon, taking the key with him.

The next year (1904), one autumn morning at 5a.m., another student woke to see a man standing by his bedside, who glided out through a shut door. Going back to sleep, he was re-awakened by loud noises which were so disconcerting that he went to a friend's room and asked him to keep him company for a while. They returned to find the rooms empty and silent. The friend left and the student re-opened his bedroom door, only to see the shadowy figure standing by his bed again. He fled his rooms in terror and refused point blank to return.

In October 1904 a student called Arthur Wade moved into the middle floor of the Old Lodge. He made friends with two students from King's College: Shane Leslie and John Capron. Shane, an Irish aristocrat, was a cousin of a young reporter and political figure called Winston Churchill. The three shared an interest in the supernatural and decided to drive the ghosts from the Old Lodge, using a translation of a medieval exorcism ceremony. They entered Arthur's rooms at 10pm at night, when John called on the spirit to appear. To their amazement a mist formed, which assumed the outline of a human body. John cried 'the thing is here', and Shane felt his hair rising. They approached the apparition together, but were forced backwards. The spectre disappeared, then re-appeared in the open doorway, as a man, visible from the knees upwards, wearing a seventeenth-century costume with a ruff collar and lace cuffs, hanging as though in punishment or torment. As the three amateur exorcists stood in terror, other students, alarmed by the noise, broke into the room, to see the entity dematerialise. John then cried that he saw it going upstairs. Re-gathering their strength, John, Arthur and Shane led the other students to the top of the stairs, where they charged into a room belonging to a medical student called Hugh Milner, a self-confessed atheist. Hugh was angry at this intrusion, but then collapsed on the floor muttering 'I am cold, I am icy cold'. Hugh's room became a scene of muddled confusion, with Shane, John and Arthur collapsing in psychical and psychological exhaustion, and the other students frightened out of their wits. Hugh, John, Arthur and Shane were led to see the college doctor and the chaplain, and the crowd gradually dispersed.

For a while the exorcism became the talk of Cambridge. People came to watch the Old Lodge, hoping to see further ghostly manifestations: practical jokers sometimes appeared at the windows dressed in sheets. The college authorities were angry about the affair, not only because they thought it brought unwelcome publicity, but also because undergraduates pulled the panelling off the Lodge walls in search of evil spirits.

Artist's impression of the 1904 ghost hunt at Corpus Christi College.

None of the participants suffered any permanent ill effects: Hugh Milner acquired a more spiritual attitude to life, John Capron became a clergyman, and Shane Leslie became a writer on the supernatural. A woman who came on the Cambridge Ghost Walk recalled how she attended a Roman Catholic Girl's School, where Shane Leslie was a regular visitor. She said he was 'a tall spare man who told us stories that gave us nightmares for weeks'.

A document describing Dr. Butts's suicide, discovered some years after the exorcism, said he had hanged himself in a doorframe by the staircase of the Master's Lodge, and was found with his knees dragging on the floor, in the place and posture in which the students saw his apparition. The sister of Dr. Robert Caldwell (master of Corpus between 1906 and 1914) found a black-framed portrait of Dr. Butts in a college attic. This was hung in the Hall: tradition holds that it fades when his ghost is active. Members of staff, including some fellows, have since claimed to have seen something moving around the Old Lodge, or running up and down a staircase there which has been sealed off for many years. In the 1930s rumours that the ghost was walking again caused the then master, William Spens, to make the somewhat unreasonable statement that anybody seeing it would be sent down! In 1967 a research fellow who had no knowledge of the ghosts spent Christmas in Corpus: on Christmas Eve he went to the kitchen under the Old Lodge, when he was frightened by the sudden appearance of a half-length figure of a man. Next year catering staff sensed a strange presence passing through the kitchen. Jeanne Youngson, a visiting university academic from New York, told Alan Murdie that she heard knocking sounds on the walls in 1994; a party of U.S. students staying at Corpus in 1999 came on the Cambridge Ghost Walk: they said they heard these, too. Further sounds were rumoured to have been heard in 2002. Altogether, the ghost of the Old Master's Lodge must be the most persistently active spirit in Cambridge!

Misfortune also befell Dr. John Spencer, who was appointed Master of Corpus in 1667. His daughter Elizabeth was born in 1672. Two years later his wife died and was buried in St. Benedict's (or 'St. Benet's') church, adjoining the college. When she was sixteen Elizabeth fell in love with a student called James Betts, but Dr. Spencer disapproved of the liaison. One day Elizabeth and James were in the Master's Lodge when they heard Dr. Spencer coming up the stairs. Fearful of Dr. Spencer's anger, James hid in a cupboard, not knowing that it could only be opened by a secret spring which could not be released from the inside. Drawing Elizabeth from the room, Dr. Spencer ordered her to accompany him on a journey which kept them away from Cambridge for the entire vacation. After their return to Corpus nobody dared to open the cupboard, terrified of what they might find and fearful that they might be accused of culpability in a horrible crime. Heartbroken at the loss of her love, Elizabeth died within a few months and was buried in St. Benet's church on 9 December 1688. Dr. Spencer's position at the University was such that nobody dared to suggest that he was in any way involved with James Betts's disappearance, but who knows what guilt he must have felt with the death of his only daughter and her lover on his conscience. Five years later he died, an unhappy and guilt-ridden man, being buried with his family in St. Benet's church on 29 May 1693. When another master was appointed he opened the cupboard and was shocked to discover a skeleton inside.

Some people might be inclined to suggest that this is a fanciful fiction, but the deaths and burials of Dr. Spencer, his wife and daughter are recorded in the parish registers of St. Benet's church. More tellingly the University archives show that James Betts, the son of a family from Norfolk, entered Corpus as an undergraduate in 1688, but disappeared from the college records without trace after one term and was never heard of again.

CLARE COLLEGE

Clare College also possessed 'a skeleton in the cupboard'. A medieval establishment, it was rebuilt over the seventeenth and early eighteenth centuries.

Robert Greene became a fellow of Clare College at the start of the eighteenth century. His career overlapped with that of Sir Isaac Newton, who was a Fellow of Trinity, although it is not known if they ever met. Robert Greene developed his own scientific theories and ideas which were wholly at variance with those of Isaac Newton. He published these in books that were generally regarded as objects of ridicule at the time and have long been forgotten. Robert Greene left his book collection and memorabilia to be placed in the college library. It was not unusual for university academics to leave such bequests to their colleges, but Robert Greene added the remarkable proviso that his body was to be dissected and his skeleton displayed in the library beside his books. He may have been uncertain that the college authorities would respect this decidedly eccentric request, since he added a codicil that if the fellows of Clare College did not want to place his skeleton on display, his collections could be offered to other Cambridge colleges, and whichever college accepted this would receive £200 (a large sum at the time) and property in his home town of Tamworth in Staffordshire. It seems that even Robert Greene's family were uncomfortable with the idea of his skeleton being placed on show, for when he died in 1730 they hurriedly organised a conventional funeral and burial.

After (very) great indecision the fellows of Clare finally decided to accept Robert Greene's legacy in 1742. (Some of the money he left was placed in trust, to fund the annual award of two *Greene Cups* to College students who have achieved distinction over the previous year.) By then Robert Greene had been dead and buried for twelve years, and nobody knew what had happened to his body (or was too anxious to find out). As a substitute, another, anonymous, skeleton was displayed in its place. Few people were very keen to see this in the library, so it was moved to a cupboard by the Hall Staircase. It disappeared from the college records in the nineteenth century. One story holds that departing students took bones as souvenirs of their stay in Cambridge until nothing was left; another possibility is that it was destroyed when a fire accidentally broke out in the staircase. Whatever happened, it appears that the college authorities made no great effort to preserve it!

A Victorian artist's impression of Dr Greene's Skeleton haunting Clare College.

A humourous portrayal of Dr Greene's Ghost.

By Victorian times there was a legend that Dr. Greene, upset by the loss of his skeleton, haunted the college in the hope that it might be restored, and that every Christmas Eve his ghost roamed the buildings and grounds, hoping to re-gather his bones, which, in view of their dispersal, must have been a rather thankless task!

SIDNEY SUSSEX COLLEGE

Further macabre tales involving disassembled bodies can be told about Sidney Sussex College, an Elizabethan college with a modern chapel, designed by John Loughborough Pearson, architect of Truro Cathedral.

In 1841 a particularly terrifying apparition was seen in the Master's Lodge, in the central block of Hall Court. On Friday 6 August 'at about the dread hour of midnight' two nursery maids were going to bed when they heard mysterious noises move around the top floor and down the stairs. The bedroom door slowly opened, and an apparition gradually materialised, taking the dim outline of a ghostly white head on a small torso, with two legs, but no arms, walking slowly forward. The maids were petrified with fear. Eventually recovering their powers of movement they ran around the shadowy apparition and fled shrieking through the door and down the stairs.

William Chafy (the Master of the college) and the rest of the household were awakened by the maids' terrified panic, and everybody in the Lodge had soon heard their story. It was suspected that they were victims of a practical joker, but all the doors and windows in the building were locked from the inside, and all the occupants had been in bed. A distinct and unusual odour permeated the air in the maids' room. Constables from Cambridge's newly established police force were called, and testified to the strange smell. The affair was considered sufficiently serious for two borough magistrates to visit the Master's Lodge, although they were unable to discover anything.

The Master's Lodge at Sidney Sussex College.

More mysterious events took place at Sidney Sussex on 1 November 1967 (just after Halloween). An undergraduate called John Emslie visited his friend Peter Knox-Shaw, who lodged off H staircase in Chapel Court. Finding the room empty, John waited for Peter's return. After a few minutes he felt a presence. Looking around he saw a shape forming in the air. He was then overcome with a horrible sensation of coldness. His neck became stiff and he found it difficult to breathe. A large mouth then began to materialise in the room, slowly coagulating into what he described as 'the most terrifying spectacle of my life': a pale, yellow emaciated head, floating in mid-air. Eventually John overcame the petrifying sensation to struggle out of the room, gasping for air as he fought the creeping paralysis from his face and throat. When Peter Knox-Shaw returned to his room, he felt inexplicably cold and frightened, and noticed a strong, putrid smell of rotting flesh. Later John Emslie returned. They knew of student pranks, but neither had heard of anything like this. Increasingly frightened, they left the room in panic, not to return that night.

Michael Howarth lived in the room above Peter Knox-Shaw. The following afternoon Michael's fiancé, Linda Nield-Siddall, was dozing on the bed in his room, when she noticed a large purple eye floating in mid-air before the door. She stood up and walked around, expecting a change of light or vision would make it vanish. Instead it stayed, disappearing and re-appearing in mid-air for ten minutes. Linda was not greatly frightened but rather unnerved, and eventually left the room.

In the following few days other students saw the eye and commented on feeling unusually cold and smelling something described as 'musty', 'earthy', 'like *Oxo*' or 'like *Spam*'. *Varsity*, the University newspaper, commented that 'one amazing thing is that everybody takes it absolutely seriously'. Psychic researchers and sightseers descended on H staircase, but the increased number of visitors and the passage of time seem to have dispersed the activity.

As far as the authors know, the 1841 sighting had been forgotten until they re-discovered it when researching Cambridge ghosts. Yet the 1841 and 1967 apparitions were remarkably similar: distorted parts of a human body materialised and vanished in mid-air, leaving a pungent odour. Possibly certain forces, as yet unknown, can re-appear in the same location over time. Although both apparitions were treated with scepticism by some people who heard about them, those who met the witnesses were convinced of their sincerity. Neither sighting can easily be dismissed as a practical joke or a hoax, and they have never been satisfactorily explained in rational terms.

During July 2002 Mexican students staying at Sidney Sussex came on the Cambridge Ghost Walk. They said they heard heavy footsteps in the corridors outside their rooms at midnight. Immediately going to look they found nothing. They did not know of the haunted reputation which the college enjoys. A college porter told Alan Murdie that in July 2007 stories were circulating around Sidney Sussex that a ghostly woman had been seen walking through a wall, and that later on bangs and thumps were heard in the room above the porter's lodge at the college entrance.

Oliver Cromwell must, for better or for worse, be the most famous person to have attended Sidney Sussex College. One of the college's claims to fame is that Oliver Cromwell's head is concealed in the college chapel.

Oliver Cromwell entered Sidney Sussex in 1616, aged seventeen, but left after one year. This may have been because of his father's death, although it was common at the time for young gentlemen to spend a short period at either Oxford or Cambridge University to develop social and academic skills without staying to complete their degrees. Little is known about Cromwell's time at Sidney Sussex: it is unclear whether he enjoyed or disliked his stay, or ever re-visited the college.

Oliver Cromwell's statue at St Ives. In 1899 there was a plan to honour the anniversary of Cromwell's birth with a monument in his native county. A statue by Frederick Pomeray was erected in St. Ives after Huntigdon declined the honour.

Oliver Cromwell's head returned to Sidney Sussex after a long, circuitous, and sometimes obscure journey. Cromwell himself died on 3 September 1658. His body was embalmed and subjected to a post-mortem examination, when the top of his skull was cut open, while death-masks were cast from his face, before burial in Westminster Abbey.

Plaque in Sidney Sussex College chapel.

After Charles II's return to England in 1660, Cromwell's body was exhumed and publicly hanged at Tyburn, London's largest gallows (on the site of Marble Arch). The corpse was then beheaded, which must have been a difficult process, as it took eight axe blows to cut the neck. The heads of those executed for crimes against the state were displayed in public places, so Cromwell's head was placed over the Houses of Parliament. (It is not known what happened to the headless corpse, the most likely possibility is that it was buried under Tyburn, although there are unsubstantiated traditions that his relations, or some of his few remaining supporters smuggled it away for a secret burial.)

There are occasional mentions of Cromwell's head being on display over the Houses of Parliament: the last such record is in 1684, when the head of Thomas Armstrong was placed alongside it, after his execution for involvement in the 'Rye House Plot' to assassinate Charles II. The head then vanishes from the historical record until the start of the eighteenth century, when it appears as an exhibit on show in a private museum owned by Claudius Du Puy, an immigrant Swiss merchant. A commonly repeated story says that it was blown off the Houses of Parliament in a storm. A sentry on duty, identified only as 'Private Barnes', picked it up and took it home in secret. Since it was announced that the person who took the head would be severely punished, Private Barnes hid it in the chimney of his house, and revealed its whereabouts to his family in a death-bed confession. While it is impossible to disprove this episode, it does not appear in print until the eighteenth century and it seems strange that the civil and military authorities would threaten to punish those who stole Cromwell's remains, when they had previously displayed no affection for his memory and failed to give him any honour. The story of a death-bed confession sounds melodramatic and fortuitous: possibly it was devised so a later owner could not be implicated in the head's theft or concealment.

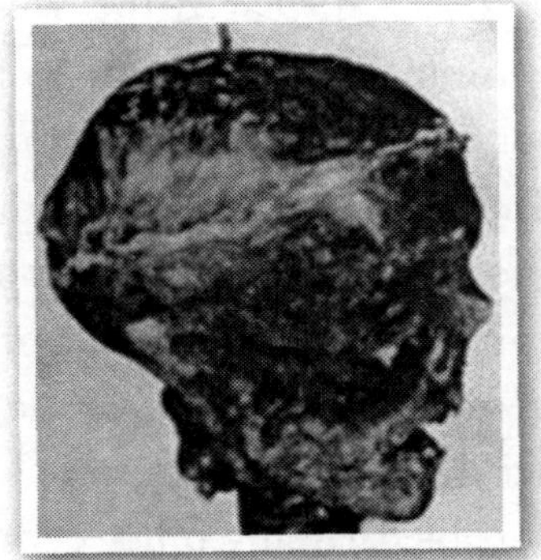
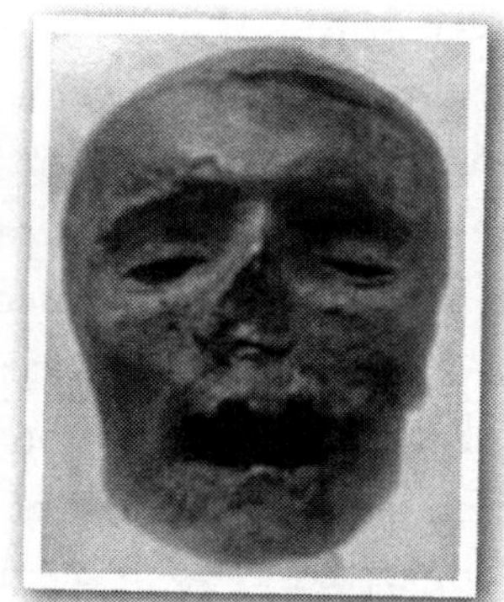

Photographs of Oliver Cromwell's head, taken in 1935.

Cromwell's head again disappears until 1775, by when it had come into the possession of Samuel Russell, a theatrical actor-manager (distantly descended from Cromwell's daughter, Frances). He gave it to a jeweller called James Cox in settlement of a debt. It must have been regarded as a desirable object, for James Cox sold it to three brothers called Hughes for £230, considerably more than a year's income for most people in England at the time. They placed it on show in London, where *The Morning Chronicle* of 18 March 1799 advertised:

> The real embalmed head of the powerful and renowned usurper, Oliver Cromwell, is now exhibited at Mead Court, Old Bond Street (where the rattlesnake was shown last year). Tickets half a crown.

Cromwell was reduced to sharing a side show with a rattlesnake. Evidently the Hughes brothers were anxious to make a return on their investment, as half a crown (two shillings and six pence, or 12½ pence in modern terms) was more than a day's pay for many workers. Perhaps not surprisingly, the exhibition failed. The Hughes Brothers gave the head to an associate called

John Cranch, who sold it to Dr. Josiah Wilkinson of Sevenoaks in Kent, from whom it was called *The Wilkinson Head* to distinguish it from other heads that were rumoured to be Cromwell's. His great-grandson, Horace Wilkinson, a clergyman, allowed it to be examined. The measurements corresponded with Cromwell's death masks; it displayed the prominent wart over the right eye which had prompted Cromwell's proverbial instruction that artists paint him 'warts and all'; and tufts of hair matched the colour of hair on these portraits. The head had been embalmed and there were axe marks on the neck. The implement impaling the neck was found to be a seventeenth century pike. Even allowing for primitive methods of forensic examination (DNA analysis and radiocarbon dating had not then been invented) and the fact that investigators were working from pre-conceived ideas, it seems impossible that any other decapitated head could display so many features by sheer chance.

When the Wilkinson family decided that Oliver Cromwell's last documented remains should finally be laid to rest they chose Sidney Sussex College for the honour. On 25 March 1960 the college chaplain conducted a ceremony, attended by the Master and three fellows of the college, along with members of the Wilkinson family, when it was interred in the chapel. There was a fear that the head might be desecrated or stolen by those who dislike Cromwell's memory, so its precise location remains a secret, known only to a few college officials.

TRINITY COLLEGE

Trinity College, the largest college in Cambridge, was founded by Henry VIII, although its size is not purely the result of Tudor royal patronage, as Henry merged two existing colleges, Michaelhouse and King's Hall, into his new foundation. Famous members of Trinity College include Sir Isaac Newton, whose memorabilia and notebooks are displayed in the college's magnificent seventeenth century Wren Library.

The Great Court at Trinity College.

William Wordsworth is one of the most famous English poets: his brother, Dr. Christopher Wordsworth, was master of Trinity College between 1820 and 1841. Once a new student asked Dr. Wordsworth for lodgings. Dr. Wordsworth obligingly directed the student to rooms which had just been vacated. After a few days the student asked to be moved elsewhere, for when he went to bed he locked the door from the inside, but every night he was awakened by the ghost of a child who wandered around the room with its hands turned outward, moaning in a disturbing fashion. Dr. Wordsworth was delighted to hear this, as the ghost had frightened previous occupants away. It was suspected that this might have been a rumour that circulated until people began to anticipate ghostly phenomena when they entered the room. So when a stranger arrived, with no previous knowledge of the college, Dr. Wordsworth could not resist the temptation to install him in the haunted room to find out if he would see the ghost. Unpleasant as the experience may have been for the student, Christopher and William Wordsworth thought this proved that ghosts did exist.

Perhaps this episode marks the beginning of Trinity College as a centre of paranormal investigation, inspiring organisations dedicated to psychic research. In 1851 Fenton Hort and Brooke Westcott, students at Trinity, formed The Ghost Club, the world's longest continually running paranormal research society. They published 750 copies of a prospectus, describing it as 'a society for the investigation of ghosts and all supernatural appearances and apparitions'. Founding members included Edward Benson, a future Archbishop of Canterbury.

Fenton Hort and Brooke Westcott would loose their original enthusiasm for ghost hunting, but went on to achieve distinction in other fields, Hort becoming a Cambridge Professor, and Westcott being appointed bishop of Durham. Nonetheless the Club's reputation sowed the seeds for several revivals to inspire generations of psychic researchers. The first revival took place in 1862, with involvement from Charles Dickens and his illustrator George Cruikshank. The Rev. Stainton Moses, a clergyman with an active interest in spiritualism, reorganised the society in 1882 as a spiritually orientated and secretive body. The club archives from Stainton Moses's period were deposited in the British Museum Library, where they were kept secret and barred to researchers for many years, until the authors were able to gain access. Members addressed each other as 'brother ghost'. Those joining became a 'ghost', and remained a member in this life and the afterlife. Any ghost infringing club rules would be 'mulcted'. The annual meeting was held on 2 November (chosen because of the French tradition of visiting cemeteries to pay respects to deceased ancestors that day), when all ghosts, living and dead, were cordially invited to attend. The Ghost Club was re-instituted a fourth time in 1938 by Harry Price, the controversial psychic investigator (best known for his books about Borley Rectory in Essex) and continues to research ghostly sightings in Great Britain.

Members of Trinity College played a key role in creating the Society For Psychical Research (S.P.R.), formed in 1882 to turn the investigation of psychic phenomena into a respectable academic discipline by scientific study. Henry Sidgwick, a fellow of Trinity and professor of moral philosophy, who had belonged to Westcott and Hort's Ghost Club, was the first president. His wife Eleanor became president of the S.P.R. in 1908. Two other members of Trinity, Frederic Myers (who devised the word 'telepathy') and Edmund Gurney, were the first secretaries. The Sidgwicks and Frederic Myers organised the Society's *Census of Hallucinations* (1894), when 17,000 people were asked if they had seen or perceived a 'ghost', (defined as a person, animal or object which had no physical reality, but was still tangible): 1,684 gave positive replies, suggesting that one person in ten sees a ghost at least once during their life. Edmund Gurney produced *Phantasms Of The Living* (1886) a study of 'crisis apparitions', when one person sees another person when they are far apart (particularly at the time of death). Frederic Myers wrote *Human Personality and its Survival of Bodily Death* (1903). These books were written in a ponderous manner, and can make difficult reading, but they were the first attempts to make a statistical analysis of the supernatural. Alan Gauld, a historian of the S.P.R. wrote 'to pass from even the ablest of previous works to *Phantasms of the Living* is like passing from a mediaeval bestiary or herbal to Linnaeus's *Systema Naturae*'. The S.P.R. archives are kept in Cambridge University Library, and were a great help in preparing this book. (See also pages 84-85.)

In 1940 Trinity College's connections with Victorian pioneers of parapsychology led it to be chosen as the home of the Perrott-Warwick scholarship, the first academic post in psychical research at a British University. This has since been held by a series of qualified investigators, who have attempted to use scientific and mathematical techniques to elucidate the nature of paranormal phenomena.

The Ghost Club and the Society For Psychical Research continue to operate, running a busy schedule of talks, lectures and investigations, regularly publishing journals and books.

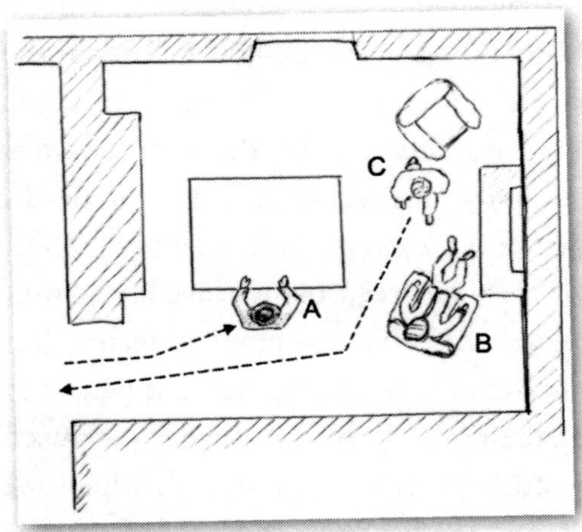

Based on a sketch by T. C. Lethbridge (C) of the appearance of a phantom (A) in the rooms of Geoffrey Walford (B) in Trinity College's New Court.

Thomas Charles Lethbridge (better known as T. C. Lethbridge) the archaeologist and parapsychologist, attended Trinity College between 1920 and 1923. His first memorable psychic encounter took place in New Court in 1922, in the rooms of a friend called 'G.W.' (Geoffrey Walford). At midnight Tom (as T. C. Lethbridge was known to his friends) got up to leave when the door opened and a man entered, wearing a top hat and fox hunting outfit (college rules obliged porters to wear top hats on Sundays). The figure walked forward to rest its hands on a table in the centre of the room. Tom said 'good evening' and left, noticing that only Geoffrey replied. Next morning Tom asked Geoffrey about the visitor. Geoffrey said nobody else had entered the room. As Tom tried to describe the figure, he realised that it appeared in black, white and grey, and made no sound. Although college porters wore top hats on Sundays, this had been a weekday, besides which no normal person would go fox hunting at midnight!

T. C. Lethbridge suspected that he had seen a ghost. This encounter led him to form the theory, that ghosts may be psychic 'photographs', in which an episode imprints itself on the scene where it occurs, but, like a film or photograph, it lacks any consciousness. This has become a popular theory among some researchers who believe that ghosts may be emotional energy imprinted on a building's physical fabric, which may, on occasions, be replayed or picked up by sensitive people. Although there is no evidence that stone, or any other chemical substance, behaves like a tape recorder, this has been dubbed 'the stone-tape theory' of ghosts (from a 1972 television drama by Nigel Kneale).

Noticing that he had seen the ghost in a room near the River Cam, T. C. Lethbridge was among the first psychic researchers to observe that ghosts often appear in damp areas, and speculate that psychic manifestations might be carried through or created by water vapour.

T. C. Lethbridge became an archaeologist in Cambridgeshire. His interest in connections between archaeology, mythology, folk customs and exploration culminated in his project to re-excavate lost hill figures on the Gogmagog Hills (see page 108). When his colleagues rejected his research in this area he abandoned Cambridge (and academia), moving to Devon to investigate parapsychology, extra-sensory perception and dowsing. While he tried to demonstrate links between these subjects and archaeology, his later research had little connection with the academic establishment. By his death in 1971 he concluded 'from a three-dimensional world I seem to have fallen through into one where there are more dimensions'. His work has since achieved cult status, and is being developed by a group of enthusiasts, *The Sons of T. C. Lethbridge*, who operate an extensive website to promote and investigate his ideas.

Alan Murdie was told that, in the winter of 1998-99 early morning cleaning staff in a modern college building heard footsteps, noticed temperature drops, and once saw an unknown man going into a room which was found to be empty. However, these manifestations ceased after a few months.

JESUS COLLEGE

Jesus College originated in the twelfth century as the Benedictine nunnery of St. Mary and St. Radegund, before being converted into a college in 1496. It retains many monastic features, including a central cloister court, while the nun's church is now the college chapel. It can therefore be argued that Jesus College has the longest continual history as a community for study and contemplation of any Cambridge college.

Predictably there are oral traditions that the College and gardens are haunted by a phantom nun, the alleged lover of a monk, the same spectre (in folklore, at least) which haunts Abbey House, one mile to the east, on the site of Barnwell Priory (see pages 75-80). Folklore also claims that a tunnel links Jesus College and Abbey House, so the nuns could hold secret liaisons with the monks of Barnwell. It should be added that no trace of any such work has ever been found, and it is unlikely that it could ever have been built, as it would run below sea level, through waterlogged soil under the floodplain of the River Cam.

Jesus College is the setting for a series of ghost stories by Arthur Gray, who entered the college in 1870 and spent seventy years there, as a student, then a fellow, and finally as master. It was claimed that by the end of his long association with the college he 'knew every stone of the college, every person in its history, every book in its library.' Arthur Gray used this knowledge to write the *History Of Jesus College* (1902) and also to compose ghost stories, written around unusual architectural features in the college or events from the college history, which he published under the pseudonym *Ingulphus* with the title *Brief Tedious Tales Of Granta And Gramarye*. *The Times* wrote 'these tales are known by heart to a small circle of faithful readers': a ghost story enthusiast might find it enjoyable to visit Jesus College with the book and read it while exploring the locations mentioned in the text.

A passage running north from the central cloister court was traditionally known as Cow Lane. Frances Wilmoth, the college archivist, suggests this was because it led to the lavatory range of the nunnery and the early college. G staircase ran eastwards off Cow Lane, leading up to an empty study: although there was no reason why this could not have housed a student or been used for college purposes, it was always kept locked. Nobody could understand why this should have been so, and Arthur Gray wrote a story to provide an explanation.

The Everlasting Club was founded in 1738 by Alan Dermot, an Irish nobleman studying at Jesus College. All members would be called Everlastings; known as Corporeal Everlastings during their lifetimes and Incorporeal Everlastings after their death. The club's annual meeting would take place on 2 November, when any Everlasting failing to attend would be punished or 'mulcted' by Alan Dermot. Charles Bellassis (a historically documented member of Jesus College) and five other Cambridge undergraduates joined the club. Meetings were notorious for drunkenness and debauchery, when all manner of riotous behaviour took place.

'Cow Lane' a passage running north from the central cloister in Jesus College.

In 1743 one Everlasting called Henry Davenport joined the army, which was then campaigning in Germany. That November Alan Dermot attended the annual meeting and said that Henry would be 'mulcted' for non-attendance. A week later the Everlastings received the news that, on 28 October, five days before the meeting, Alan Dermot had fought a duel with somebody who objected to is wicked ways. Alan had lost the duel and been killed. He had attended the meeting as an *Incorporeal Everlasting*! They then received the news that Henry Davenport had been killed by a cannon ball on 3 November. Alan Dermot could carry out punishments from beyond the grave!

Over the next few years the other Everlastings died in mysterious circumstances. By 1766 only Charles Bellassis was left. On November 2 he locked himself into his study at the head of G staircase. From ten o'clock that night there was a hideous uproar in Charles Bellassis's study. 'Blasphemous outcries and ribald songs, such as had not been heard for twenty years aroused from sleep or study the occupants of the court.' At midnight all noise ceased and the lights in the study went out. Next morning Charles failed to open the study door. Members of the college broke the door open and found the room in total chaos, with books and furniture strewn everywhere and glasses and bottles littering the floor. In the centre of the room there was a table surrounded by seven chairs. Six were empty, but in the seventh sat the dead body of Charles Bellassis. He head was thrown back and his face paralysed in an expression of horrified terror. On the table lay the register of the Everlasting Club, signed by all seven original members in their own handwriting, with a final message that Charles Bellassis had been mulcted for failing to provide proper hospitality. The study was locked and never used again. Few people dared to enter, but ever since, every 2 November, from ten o'clock until midnight, the sound of drunken revelry echoes down G staircase and along Cow Lane as it had in the days of the Everlasting Club.

The story proved so popular that it quickly passed into Cambridge folklore, being mentioned in Arthur Gray's history of the college when it was updated for re-publication in 1979, even though Charles Bellassis' study was re-opened in 1924, and no ghostly happenings have taken place there since, despite the best hopes that they might. In 1977 a student social club called The Jesus Old Contemptibles honoured the Everlasting Club by holding a meal there on 2 November. Hopefully they displayed more decorous conduct than Alan Dermot and his companions, but no Everlastings appeared in either corporeal or incorporeal form to join in, which may have been just as well considering what had happened to Charles Bellassis in 1766.

Sketch of the entry to the study where the Everlasting Club had their final meeting.

The rules of the Everlasting Club and the Ghost Club from Trinity College, as reconstituted in 1882, bear similarities (see pages 32-3). All who joined were called 'ghosts' and remained members in this life and the afterlife. The annual meeting was held on 2 November, when all members, living and dead, were cordially invited to attend. Another telling detail was the rule that any 'ghost' infringing club rules would be 'mulcted'. It is impossible to avoid the conclusion that the tale of *The Everlasting Club* was inspired by the Ghost Club.

CHRIST'S COLLEGE

Christ's College was set up in 1505 by Henry VII's mother, Margaret Beaufort. There are rumours that Lady Margaret's ghost walks here, although it is uncertain if there are any documented sightings. Charles Darwin was perhaps its most famous student: his former rooms are now open to the public. The college's attractions include the seventeenth century Fellow's Building and the exceptionally beautiful Fellow's Garden (containing two mulberry trees which are traditionally associated with another famous student, the poet John Milton).

The Fellow's Garden is known for a fictional ghost: Christopher Round, the phantom don, whose story was written in 1918, by Alfred Ponsford Baker, a college tutor, in a novella entitled *A College Mystery*, which tells how, in the nineteenth century Christopher Round and Philip Collier lodged on staircase A of the Fellows Building. Christopher resented Philip, whose work attracted higher praise. They met a woman called Mary Clifford: Christopher fell in love with her, but she chose Philip's proposal of marriage. Philip was then observed to be unkempt and dishevelled, smelling of spirits, reeling and staggering in an ungainly manner, and it was rumoured that he was a drunkard. One night Christopher was walking past the pond in the Fellow's Garden when Philip staggered past and fell headlong into the water. Christopher noticed a pole lying on the ground: overcome with anger and jealousy he raised the pole and furiously struck at Philip again and again. Philip's dead body was found next morning. Christopher then discovered that Mary Clifford was suffering from a serious, and potentially fatal illness, but that her life might have been saved by an operation. Philip was taking drugs and anaesthetics in an attempt to find a way to treat her illness: he was not drinking, but conducting a private medical experiment to save Mary's life. Christopher Round spent the rest of his life wracked by guilt, he died an unhappy man, since when, every 29 May, his ghost has walked down staircase A and across the Fellows' Garden, wearing old-fashioned clothes and conveying an air of care and unhappiness.

Arthur Ponsford Baker died in 1919, and is commemorated by a plaque in the college chapel. Christopher Round's ghost has passed into Cambridge folklore. *A College Mystery* was re-published by Back-In-Print Books in 2004, and is now available in most Cambridge bookshops. Richard Reynolds of Heffers, the long-established Cambridge bookshop, helped in the re-publication after hearing stories of people who suffered a frightening and sleepless night in the Fellows Building, only to be told

The Fellow's Building at Christ's College; staircase A, haunted by Christopher Round's ghost, extends behind the smaller door to the left.

the story of Christopher Round afterwards. In 1998 Michael Wyatt, a graduate of Christ's, contacted the college to suggest hat there may have been a factual basis to the story of the Fellows' Building ghost. His father, Travers Wyatt, had previously been a member of the college. Later one May in about 1930 the Wyatt family received a visit from a distant cousin, Sam Wheeler, a former naval officer who had served at the battle of Jutland. The Wyatt family did not have a spare room in their house, so they arranged for Uncle Sam to stay in the Fellows' Building. By apparent co-incidence Uncle Sam was given the room where Alfred Baker had located Christopher Round's apartments, and he stayed there on 29 May, the day when Christopher Round's ghost was supposed to walk. Next morning Uncle Samuel appeared white-faced to say he had not slept for constant banging in the room and footsteps running around outside. Autosuggestion or temperature changes (it was a hot summer night) might have been to blame, but, although the Wyatt family were fully acquainted with the story of Christopher Round they had always regarded it as nothing more than a story, besides which they had not mentioned the tale to Uncle Samuel, who, after his naval career, was hardly the sort of person to scare easily. Is staircase *A* of the Fellow's Building susceptible to phenomena after all?

ST JOHN'S COLLEGE

Turret in the Second Court of St John's College, haunted by Dr James Wood.

As well as Christ's College, Lady Margaret Beaufort also established St. John's College in 1511. Its famous students include the Elizabethan alchemist and occultist, John Dee. Much of the First Court dates from Margaret Beaufort's time, apart from the unusually large Victorian college chapel, whose attractions include a 'cadaver memorial' of Hugh Ashton, an early fellow, saved from the medieval chapel, showing him as the emaciated, skeletal corpse that he would become after death. St. John's College was extended with the Elizabethan Second Court; in the Victorian era it expanded across the Cam, access to the new buildings being by a covered stone bridge, universally known as 'The Bridge Of Sighs'.

Alan Murdie heard a story that a college stable block burned down on 3 August, and every year, on the anniversary of the fire, the crackling sounds of burning and the neighing of horses can be heard, accompanied by the acrid smell of smoke.

Dr James Wood's ghost is said to appear on O staircase in the turret in the southeast corner of the Second Court. A Lancashire weaver's son, James won a place at the college in 1778, where he occupied a garret leading off O staircase. Too poor to afford a fire, or even candles, at night he studied on the staircase by the glow of the rush candle in the passage and the light coming from under wealthier students' doors, his feet wrapped in straw to protect them from the cold. When James took his degree he achieved the prestigious title of Senior Wrangler, awarded to the student who achieved the top marks of that year. He became a fellow, and later master of St. John's. On his death he left a large fortune which he bequeathed to his college. Yet the memory of his early days would never leave him, and his ghost can still be seen on the staircase where he worked as a poor student.

In 1746 St. John's College was the setting for a historically documented disaster. James Ashton, a newly arrived student, was found to have died in his rooms in the First Court. His body displayed several deep wounds, and there were broken items nearby. It was unclear if this was a horrifying freak accident, a suicide, or a murder. Many people favoured the latter option, and suspicion fell on another student, John Brinkley, with whom James was known to be well-acquainted, and who was seen with him on the night of his death. John Brinkley was taken for trial, but found not guilty. However, there were some inconsistencies in his testimony, and not all suspicions were allayed. John Brinkley left Cambridge soon afterwards, and wholly disappears from history. Although the location of James Ashton's rooms within the First Court is not known, in 2001 a fellow of St. John's speculated that certain inexplicable noises and movements in and around the college library may have been the death being re-enacted.

In 2000 Alan Murdie was led to doubt the authenticity of some reported activity at St. John's College, after meeting a retired college porter who confessed that during his thirty years service he patrolled the college late at night, rattling a large chain and making groaning noises. Perhaps occasional reports of manifestations may owe more to the nocturnal activities of this gentleman than any paranormal cause!

EMMANUEL COLLEGE

Emmanuel College was founded in 1584 on the site of a Dominican friary. Although most of the college buildings post-date the establishment of the college, including the chapel, which was designed by Christopher Wren, it is tempting to think that the front court was adapted from the friar's cloister. In view of the extensive folklore about secret underground tunnels in Cambridge, it may be amusing to find that Emmanuel College does contain a subterranean passage, usually accessible to visitors, connecting the main college with the North Court, on the opposite side of Emmanuel Street.

There was a Victorian haunting in Emmanuel House, on the college's eastern perimeter, facing Parker Street. The Harris family, who lived there from 1867, often heard footsteps running along empty passageways. Emily Harris, the mother of the family, was in bed when she saw a woman wearing a grey veil standing beside her. Thinking it might be a trick of the light she moved around in the bed, but the figure remained stationary, yet quite distinct. At this point she dived under the bedclothes, too frightened even to scream! When she eventually gathered enough courage to look out again the woman had vanished. On employing a young boy as a servant the Harris family were careful not to tell him that their house was haunted, but one morning, a few days after his arrival, he was heard screaming. The whole household ran to find him huddled on the floor in a terrified heap, crying that he had just seen a ghost. His description corresponded exactly with the figure Emily Harris had seen.

Miss Bowen, the next tenant, continued to hear footsteps, as did her maid, Kate. The building then became a girl's boarding school. In 1884 a teacher called Miss Bellamy, who was respected as a formidable, no-nonsense schoolmistress, was standing in the kitchen when a strange woman descended the stairs and crossed the hall. Miss Bellamy was puzzled, for the woman had not been seen to enter the house, appeared unfamiliar, and was gliding along the floor without making any noise or movement, apparently unaware of being watched. The woman passed from view into the dining room. Miss Bellamy went straight after her, but the woman had vanished, and nobody had seen her leave the house. She did not find out that Emmanuel House was supposed to be haunted until some years later.

The Harris family knew of a vague tradition that three previous occupants had committed suicide. There was a possibility that some disturbing events had affected the building, but they knew little about these. The building was demolished in 1893, and replaced by the present Emmanuel House, and no ghostly activity has been noted on the site since.

ST. CATHERINE'S COLLEGE

St. Catherine's College, a medieval establishment, was wholly rebuilt between 1673 and 1704 around the large Main Court (slightly misnamed, as the east side, facing Trumpington Street, is open to the road). During the rebuilding it expanded over the site of the premises of the Cambridge tradesman, Thomas Hobson, who, a century previously, had become legendary for business acumen by carrying people and goods between Cambridge and London. Thomas Hobson worked his horses in strict rotation, to ensure that none were underworked or overworked. Every customer, without exception, was obliged to hire the horse nearest the stable door, giving rise to the expression 'Hobson's choice', meaning 'take it or leave it'. In 1930 a northern extension of St Catherine's College, facing Trumpington Street, was built over the site of his stables and called The Hobson Building in his memory.

Although one might expect ghosts to appear within Cambridge University's many historic buildings, it is paradoxical that, within a year of its opening, the Hobson Building was said to be haunted. The college magazine reported:

> Rumour has it that a ghost may be heard, already, prowling in the small hours on the staircases of Hobson's Building. And, if this is so, it can, of course, be none other than the Cambridge carrier's. Certainly the new addition to the College is worthy in every respect of the old building which it flanks, and, if the ghost elects to walk there, rather than in the mysterious rooms whose windows are above the chapel roof, *Hobson's choice* is, in this case, proof of commendable discrimination.

Thomas Hobson had died in 1631 and been buried in St. Benet's Church. It is uncertain whether his ghost might wish to return to a location which would have changed beyond recognition over three hundred years (unless he felt honoured that St. Catherine's college had named a building after him). Little is known about the alleged haunting: it might only have been random anomalous phenomena, or even unsubstantiated rumour, and may have ceased after a short while, as the Hobson Building is not now thought to be haunted.

One intriguing detail of the above account is the reference to 'the mysterious rooms whose windows are above the chapel roof'. The chapel stands on the north side of Main Court: the attic rooms above it are known as 'Sky Hall'. In 1980, Mr. S. J. Alderton, an elderly member of staff, recalled college life at the start of the century:

> These were the days of oil lamps and candles and the Sky Hall Ghost. One Mr R. A. Kennedy used to sleep with a pistol under his pillow. He was also a collector of lamp-post numbers, door knockers etc… I had a scare on going up Sky Hall one evening. Everything was in darkness; no light

on the staircase or in the room when I reached the top, just something white through the wide open door. I was scared stiff, but decided to investigate and found it to be a surplice hanging on the wide open bedroom door.

The Main Court at St Catherine's College. The taller range contains the chapel (foreground) and student accommodation (to the back). The attic floor of this wing, behind the five western dormer windows, is known as 'Sky Hall'. The three dormer windows above the chapel are dummies, added for symmetry.

Clearly the attic known as Sky Hall was once thought to have been haunted. As a Cambridge undergraduate, psychical researcher Tony Cornell met Dr. William Henry Samuel Jones, a senior fellow of St. Catherine's. Known as 'Malaria Jones' from his book *Malaria And Greek History* (1918), he also wrote *The Story Of St. Catherine's College* (1951). Dr. Jones told Tony Cornell the story of the Sky Hall Ghost.

In 1927 a new student (name withheld) was given accommodation in Sky Hall. A scholarship student from a poor family, he was willing to stay there because it had a low rent. It contained a large fireplace and a heavy wooden chair. Like most freshmen, he took up lodgings in autumn, so his first term co-incided with the onset of winter, and he had to maintain a fire to keep himself warm. As time passed he began to see an old man sitting in the chair, with grey hair and a long beard, wearing a red robe and black boots, staring intently at the fire. Sometimes the old man turned to face him while pointing to the fire. One night, finding the heat of the fire too intense and the old man's presence too much to bear, he jumped out of bed, picked up a jug of water and threw it on the fire. He then dozed fitfully, and woke to see the old man staring accusingly, pointing at the fire grate. The following night he lit a large fire: too apprehensive to sleep properly, he woke to see the man turned away, hands outstretched towards the roaring blaze. Next morning he received two letters saying he had been allocated a new room, and his tutor urgently wished to see him. His tutor listened sympathetically to the story of the old man's ghost, and said that Sky Hall had always been an unpopular lodging. Unpleasant rumours about the place had circulated, but he was asked not to disclose these for the sake of the college's honour and reputation. After moving to another room he became a successful student, gained a good degree, and had a distinguished adult career. There may have been a possibility that somebody died of hypothermia in Sky Hall, but the student was never sure.

Dr. Jones also told Tony Cornell how, in 1923, he occupied rooms at the foot of the southwest staircase in Main Court. Having to leave Cambridge for several days, he let a Board of Education Inspector (whose name he also withheld) stay there while attending a conference at Cambridge. After one night the inspector woke to find furniture moved and a sideboard jammed against the door. Suspecting that somebody was playing tricks, the next night he locked the door and windows. He was twice wakened by bumping on the wall and his bed moving: next morning he found his bed had moved, as had items of furniture, which he found too heavy to reposition, and his clothes were thrown around. That night he found all the furniture had been replaced apart from the sideboard. He tried to sleep, but his bed shook and the bedclothes flapped, while the furniture creaked and the sideboard slid backwards and forwards. In panic and fear he ran to a colleague's rooms and spent the rest of the night there. Next morning the room was in chaos with the bed overturned. Dr. Jones saw this disorder: it took three men to return the sideboard to its original position. Dr. Jones occupied the rooms for several more years, but nothing untoward took place there again, nor, as far as was known, did anything remotely similar befall the inspector. Dr. Jones was told that about ten or twelve years previously a college servant had committed suicide in the room at about the same date as the inspector's stay.

The Main Court of St Catherine's College, facing west. The attic windows of 'Sky Hall' can be seen to the north (right); rooms in the south west corner (to the left) saw poltergeist activity in 1923.

Staircase E, which connects to the neighbouring King's College, may have had a reputation as a haunted part of the college, because when it was rebuilt in 1965 the college magazine reported:

> E staircase, which may or may not have foundations, and from which during the course of the year most of the residents have been evacuated… has now to be forcibly dismantled, together with all its associations, its inscribed plate-glass windows, its ghost lore, and its all-pervasive medieval smells.

PETERHOUSE COLLEGE

The Old Court Peterhouse College, facing east. The bay window of the thirteenth century hall extends from the south range (right); the Combination Room is behind the four ground floor windows beyond this. The chapel stands in the centre of the far range.

Peterhouse College, the oldest Cambridge college, founded in 1284, is centred on The Old Court: the thirteenth century Hall and the adjoining parlour, on the south side of the Old Court, are the oldest purpose-built college buildings in Cambridge; the seventeenth century college chapel stands centrally on the east of the court.

F staircase, in the south west corner of the Old Court (supposedly haunted by a blue lady).

In the mid-twentieth century a story circulated that a blue lady haunted F staircase, by the Hall and Parlour. She was said to have been associated with Peterhouse in Victorian times, although her identity was uncertain.

The churchyard of Little St. Mary's church adjoins Peterhouse to the north: long disused for burials, this is now one of the most overgrown parts of the city centre. The college's north face, overlooking the churchyard, faces away from the sun for most of the day, and can appear overcast. The passage between Little St. Mary's Lane and the college's north entrance can have a gloomy atmosphere, and a Dean once performed an exorcism to remove a dark presence from the corner overlooking the churchyard. Members of college staff have told the authors that it resembled a man crouching down by or on the gateway, almost as though he was pretending to be a cat or panther, staring intently at something in the graveyard. Many who experienced this presence found it evil, receiving feelings of sickness and revulsion.

The gloomy north entrance to Peterhouse College.

Some people attending the Cambridge Ghost Walk have said that as children in the early 1960s they were warned away from the area; others who are unfamiliar with Cambridge feel uneasy there: on 1 November 1998 an Italian psychic accompanying a Ghost Club visit experienced an adverse reaction. A few people being told about the place have even thought they were touched, felt discomfort in their heads or limbs, and been impelled to leave the spot, or even cry, claiming a malign presence was overcoming them. However, some extreme reactions could be auto-suggestion, since similar effects can be triggered by a dramatic stage play or film with a supernatural theme.

The Combination Room in Peterhouse College.

Over 1997 ghosts were seen in the fifteenth century Combination Room, which is linked to the thirteenth century Hall by a passage that terminates in a bell-tower containing a spiral staircase, overlooking the college gardens. At 9.30pm on 17 April two college waiters, Paul Davies and Matthew Speller, descended this staircase. As they entered the Combination Room a white, hooded figure materialised in the centre of the room, glided to the bay window in the south wall, and disappeared. At the same time Paul and Matthew heard knocking from the panelling and rattling on the doors. Shaken by the experience, they told Dr. Graham Ward, the Dean. It turned out that they were not the first people to have experienced strange phenomena there, for other members of the catering staff began to report that they had noticed sudden temperature drops in the Combination Room and heard knocking behind the panelling.

On the evening of 27 October Dr. Graham Ward was presiding over an official function in the Hall. At 8.30 Paul Davies again entered the Combination Room. It was well lit, and two coal fires were blazing in the grates. Once more he was dumbstruck as the white figure materialised in the centre of the room. Paul called Matthew Speller and the college butler, Mark Cooke, who rushed in to see the figure gliding to the bay window. As before they heard knocking on the walls and rattling on the doors. They rushed into the Hall to tell Dr. Ward that the ghost had appeared again. It rather broke University protocol for the Dean to leave the Hall during an official function, but Dr. Ward was anxious to see the ghost, and he left to go into the Combination Room. By the time that he entered the ghost had vanished, but he noticed that the room had become cold, despite two roaring fires. Dr. Ward vouched for the integrity of Paul Davies, Matthew Speller and Mark Cooke, and the look of stark terror on their faces after the sightings. It was noted that, allowing for the fact that the clocks are moved back one hour for winter, both appearances occurred at the same time.

Early in December the college bursar, Andrew Murison, went into the Combination Room. Going to take some fruit from a fruit bowl be heard knocking on the walls and sensed a cold, clammy presence behind him. He turned around to see a small man wearing a jacket with a wide collar, and holding a large hat. Andrew thought it was a member of the college staff until he noticed the figure's unusual costume. After a few seconds it quietly disappeared in front of him. Andrew then noticed that the room had become very cold, even though an open fire was burning in the grate.

The ghost came to media attention in December 1997, when it was reported in several national newspapers, on BBC Radio Four, and even the television news. There were suggestions that it was James Dawes, a fellow who hanged himself in 1789, after involvement in an election scandal, when he became very unpopular after supporting the appointment of an unpopular master. James Dawes's obituary in *The Gentleman's Magazine*, a London journal, said he hanged himself from a bell-rope in the college chapel. However, the bell ropes are hung in a space which is only ten feet high, and anybody pulling them would only be lowered on to the floor, while ringing the bell, thus rousing the entire college. And, although it is hard to understand the ways of a ghost, why would James Dawes haunt the Combination Room if he died in the college chapel? Then in November

The Gentleman's Magazine published a retraction, altering this:

> Mr. Dawes was not found in the college chapel, but in a neglected turret in the garden; a place which, in happier times, he had been heard to mention as well situated for such a purpose as he himself unfortunately effected.

James Dawes did not hang himself in the college chapel, as is often believed, but in the turret adjoining the passage from the Combination Room, a location in which he had previously expressed a morbid interest. This would explain why his ghost was seen near here.

Turret in the south range of Peterhouse College where James Dawes hanged himself in 1789. The Combination Room stands on the ground floor, behind the bay window.

These three appearances of a ghost in Peterhouse College in one year, witnessed by several conscientious members of staff, represent one of the most striking examples of a haunting in Britain in modern times.

CAMBRIDGE CITY CENTRE GHOSTS

THE RAINBOW VEGETARIAN RESTAURANT

While the colleges of Cambridge University are the setting for some intriguing ghost stories, paranormal activity has been observed elsewhere in the city centre. The Rainbow Vegetarian Restaurant, at 9 King's Parade, opened in 1987 in the cellar of a range of seventeenth century buildings opposite King's College. It has won awards for hospitality and cuisine, and also enjoys the further distinction of being the United Kingdom's only haunted vegetarian restaurant. The ghost is believed to be Sarah (better known as Sadie) Barnet, a Cambridge landlady who owned the building for fifty years and enjoyed a fearsome reputation for disciplining student lodgers with a strict regime, curbing anything she considered unacceptable behaviour on her premises (although the rumour that she murdered her first husband and buried him in the wall of the Rainbow was simply malicious gossip). In later years, Sadie's former student lodgers recalled her eccentricities with nostalgic affection and her passing on 15 August 1991 was marked with an obituary in the *Daily Telegraph.*

Proprietor Sharon Meijland says that she and other staff have sensed two presences in the cellar restaurant. Once, at 10pm, in early August 2003 she was locking up when she felt a like physical push as though she was being forced from the building. As may be imagined, this quite unnerved her and for a period she would not enter her restaurant. In August 2008 Sharon's son, Joshua, glimpsed a figure which he thought was a customer near the stairs; he looked again a few seconds later and no-one was present. Both sightings were near the anniversary of Sadie's death. More often footsteps have been heard descending the stairs, typically at about 10pm, when the premises are quiet. Sometimes they finish with a knocking at the door, or even the sound of a customer in the restaurant area coughing for attention. But when the staff look nobody is there.

Another old lady who lived in rooms above the restaurant wore perfume and walked with a stick. People have heard the tapping, like a walking stick, and smelt perfume from the front area of the restaurant, under her house: she was once seen by a chef, who described her, even though he had never previously been told about her or even seen her picture.

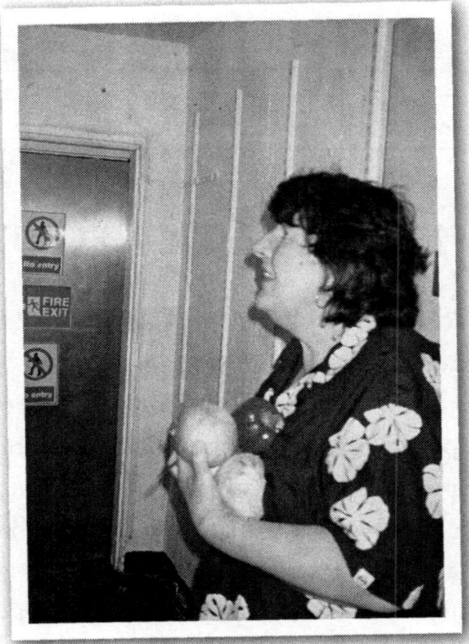

Sharon Meijland indicating a focus of paranormal activity in the Rainbow vegetarian restaurant.

The Ghost Club conducted ghostwatches in the restaurant. Nothing conclusive was observed, although once the lights failed for about half an hour. Electrical anomalies are frequently reported in haunted houses, but it must be admitted they may arise from mundane causes. Renovation and the replacement of old wall insulation may have put an end to the hauntings.

JIM GARRAGHY'S FUDGE KITCHEN

Jim Garraghy's Fudge Kitchen stands at 11 King's Parade. Laura Cox, a member of staff, told Alan Murdie that at about 6pm on 22 October 2005 she had closed the shop and gone to the cellar when she heard footsteps entering the shop floor above. Thinking it was a late customer she went upstairs to find the shop empty and the front door locked. The incident was more puzzling than frightening. Laura said that staff using a computer in the basement have complained of a sensation of a presence immediately behind them or creeping up on them.

THE HAUNTED BOOKSHOP

The Haunted Bookshop, a second hand and antiquarian bookstore at 9 St. Edward's Passage, is the only building in Cambridge that openly advertises the presence of a ghost. It acquired its name in 1986 after the then proprietor saw a charming apparition at the head of the stairs: a young girl with long, flowing fair hair. Sarah Key, the present owner, saw her on the stairs in 1994. Other members of staff have seen her, too: some have followed the girl upstairs, believing her to be a customer, only to find the upper floor empty. Staff at the Indigo Restaurant next door have heard noises from the bookshop early in the evening when it is closed. Dating from the eighteenth century, the building was once a beer shop (called 'The Red House'). It was also student accommodation for many years. Sarah Key said 'I am sure that the ghost is connected with a previous occupier, but who, what and when remains a mystery'. In 1997 *The Y Files*, a cable channel programme, made a broadcast from the shop in which a psychic sensed a female presence that she identified as benign. Alan Hudleston, a shop assistant, said the ghost's appearances are accompanied by the smell of violets. Evidently this ghost need not be feared: those seeing her may find it a pleasant experience.

The display window at The Haunted Bookshop.

THE INDIGO COFFEE HOUSE

St Edward's Passage: The Indigo Coffee House can be seen in the foreground, 'The Haunted Bookshop' stands next door.

The Indigo Coffee House stands next door to the Haunted Bookshop at 8 St. Edward's Passage. The city's smallest independent café, it opened in 1999 and has proved popular with students and visitors. The staff have told Alan Murdie how, one day in the summer of 2002, they came in, went down into the cellar kitchen and found all the marshmallows placed on the steps! After this there were strange object movements, including furniture being piled up by itself. The assistant manager had the keys to the building and at weekends would sometimes come in to check the premises, relax, and sleep on the sofa in preference to cycling home. One night he was calmly smoking a cigarette on the sofa when two tea spoons rose in the air, hovered for a moment, came together with an audible click and tumbled to the floor. He left the Indigo Coffee House at great speed and would not re-enter after dark. Soon afterwards he left to work at the neighbouring Arts Theatre.

THE OLD BOROUGH LIBRARY

Entrance to Cambridge's Victorian Borough Library where Alan Murdie had a paranormal experience in 2010.

The Victorian Borough Library was built in 1862 at the corner of Peas Hill and Wheeler Street. John Pink, the first borough librarian, held the post until 1905. His ghost was supposed to haunt the building: when caretakers heard the floors creaking at night they said it was John Pink, still going on his rounds. He was reputedly seen by a caretaker in 1970, who identified him from old pictures and portraits. After a new library was opened in Lion Yard in 1975 the building was converted into a tourist information centre. When Alan Murdie was talking about ghosts on Radio Cambridgeshire in 1998 a former library service employee telephoned to say that he saw John Pink's ghost in the building in 1972. In August 1998 a tourist information worker told Alan Murdie that, shortly after it opened, footsteps had been heard there. The building would be locked at night, but when staff arrived next morning objects had inexplicably moved. Michael Petty, the former local studies librarian, was asked for a comment. He confirmed that staff were aware of the story for as long as the building had been a library, and added that the head caretaker had been convinced that John Pink was responsible for continued clicking and creaking. On 8 June 2000 Alan Murdie was conducting the Cambridge Ghost Walk for a party of about a dozen people. At 9pm he was outside the main doors, talking about the hauntings, when they shook for several seconds in front of the entire party. On making enquiries at the Tourist Information Office the next day Alan was assured that the staff all left around 6pm, leaving the building locked. In 2010 the building was converted into a restaurant. It will be interesting to see if further manifestations are reported.

THE EAGLE PUB

The Eagle pub, Benet Street.

Two separate people attending the Cambridge Ghost Walk told Alan Murdie about a girl in Victorian dress who appeared on the staircase in The Eagle pub in Benet Street. In the winter of 1959 she was seen in a glowing light, holding a lighted candle in a silver candlestick; in 1977 she appeared dressed in black. Alan Murdie has also heard an oral tradition that the building is haunted by two young boys who died mysteriously there. Could these children have met with a tragic experience that impressed itself on the building? A table in The Eagle is said to tilt up and down at unexpected moments. Witnesses might not necessarily be considered the most reliable, as they may have been consuming alcohol when this occurs, but those enjoying a drink in this pub had best hold their glasses tightly, or they may find themselves upset by spirits in more ways than one!

THE PHANTOM PICTURE

Trumpington Street is the setting for the story of The Phantom Picture. Originally published in 1937 in a short-lived local magazine called *The Cam,* this is unique in the annals of psychic research, for the authors can find no similar episode in any factual or fictional ghost story. Enid Porter saw it at the very least as a genuine piece of Cambridge folklore.

At the end of the nineteenth century a wealthy woman saw a house in Trumpington Street advertised for sale, and went to view it with the possible intention of purchase. A maid showed the woman into a ground floor sitting room and went to call the mistress. Looking around the room, the woman saw the portrait of a lady hanging above the mantelpiece. The sitter wore a bright green dress and a hat with a red feather, but the woman was alarmed by the expression on the sitter's face, which was extremely sinister and unpleasant. The proprietor came downstairs and took the woman into the drawing room to discuss purchase. At the end of the conversation the owner said:

'I think perhaps I ought to tell you that there is a silly story about the house being haunted, but I don't suppose that will affect your decision.'

Intrigued, the woman asked if anybody had seen the ghost. The homeowner replied that the ghost was supposed to take the appearance of a woman wearing a bright green dress and a hat with a red feather.

'Oh', the woman replied, 'you mean the lady whose portrait hangs over the mantelpiece in the room I was first shown into?'

'Portrait?' returned the startled homeowner, 'there is no portrait in that room!'

They returned to the sitting room. Hanging above the mantelpiece was a country landscape. The woman had seen a ghost, not in the shape of a living person, but in the form of an oil painting.

THE HAUNTED PHOTOGRAPHIC STUDIO

The Jet Photographic Studios stands at 1B Botolph Lane. There is a central staircase leading upstairs at the back of the shop. In 2009 John Thompson, the present proprietor, told Robert Halliday that an assistant called Laura Carlton saw a young girl in a Victorian costume walk down the stairs and continue past her into the side room on the ground floor. Laura was struck by the girl's Victorian button up boots, which was a telling detail, as the building was a shoeshop in Victorian times. John himself had felt something walk down the stairs and past him, although he did not see it.

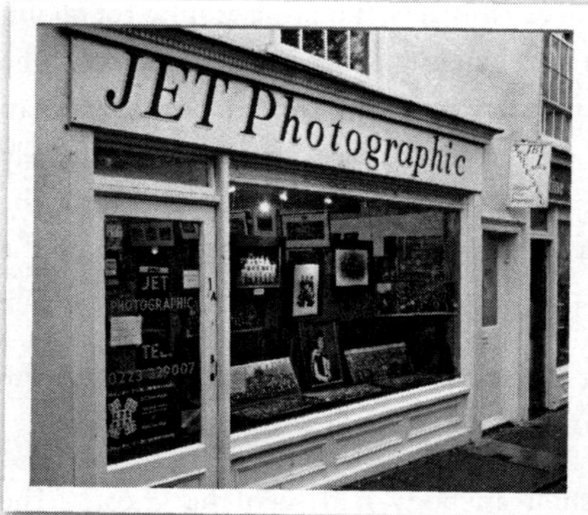

The photographic studio at 1b Botolph Lane: ghosts have been spotted on the central staircase.

Under previous management, when the business operated as *The Cambridge Photographic Studio*, there were rumours that staff saw a person's feet going up the stairs, but the figure vanished as soon as they caught sight of it. Interestingly this figure was considered to be male, but the face was not seen because of the apparition's position on the stairs.

SILVER STREET

Silver Street, facing West.

On the evening of 21 November 1954 a student walked west down Silver Street to Queen's College. Colleges then operated a curfew and students locked out after closing time could be disciplined and fined. All students broke curfew at some time and tried to re-enter their college by devious methods: this student planned to wait until Silver Street was empty and climb over the perimeter wall. It was a clear night, and a street light was working. As he came within sight of the *Anchor* pub he saw an old man in front of him, with long, thinning silver hair, wearing a morning coat, walking down the street with a stooped posture, the hands clasped behind the back. The student followed the old man for a minute, but when he was two paces away the old man simply vanished! Although surprised, the student (who had no previous interest in ghosts or the paranormal) scaled the wall and ran to his rooms, where he immediately wrote an account of his experience. He forwarded it to local members of the Society For Psychical Research (requesting anonymity as he was in breach of college regulations at the time) and subsequently met the Society's president, who was convinced of his sincerity.

5 PEMBROKE STREET

5 Pembroke Street.

In 2007 Robert Halliday met Kathy Skin of Cambridge. A member of the Women's Royal Naval Service (or 'Wrens' as they were popularly known) during the Second World War, she came home on leave to 5 Pembroke Street, a furnished home her mother leased from Pembroke College. Sleeping in a Victorian bed in a top floor bedroom, she woke in the night to see a young man looking at her. A handsome youth, aged about eighteen or nineteen, about five foot ten or eleven tall, with a long white face, pale white skin, long dark hair and unusually long thin hands and fingers, he wore a long dark jacket, a white collar and a bootlace tie. Kathy saw him as a 'boy who wasn't a boy'. He placed his hands on her, but she did not feel them. His expression was initially one of amazement which turned to great fright. Kathy said: 'You're in the wrong room' and pushed at him:

her hands went through him, but he did not move. She yelled and got up to put the light on, forgetting the blackout regulations. She then looked around and could not see anything, when a voice from the street called 'Put that light out'.

Kathy's mother, who slept in the basement, heard her yell, and came to tell her to come down. Kathy described what she had seen over a cup of tea. Her mother said 'Don't be worried, I've seen him many times myself.' Mrs. Skin had first seen him at the top of the stairs coming down from the bedroom, and had spoken to him, but he walked through her, whereupon she fainted. Mrs. Skin had often seen him after that. Sometimes he wore a gown, at other times a mortarboard hat. (At that time Cambridge students had to wear academic robes.) Sometimes he was with another boy: her mother thought he was an Edwardian youth. Mrs. Skin investigated and found that four young men committed suicide at the house over ten years. Kathy believed the boy she saw had taken an overdose, and was not looking at her, but his body; she may have been sleeping in his bed.

Kathy said that while her mother continued to see the ghost, she never saw it again herself, although she would recognise the figure to that day. After the war her family moved to South Africa, where they received a nasty letter from the next tenants complaining they had not been told that the house was haunted. Yet Kathy said that the house always seemed to have 'such a lovely atmosphere'; she felt happy and comfortable there, and she thought all the young men who previously lived there combined to make it a happy place.

LITTLE ST. MARY'S LANE

Little St Mary's Lane from the churchyard.

A row of attractive, historic buildings in Little St. Mary's Lane overlooks Little St. Mary's churchyard and Peterhouse College's north face. One house, whose location the University authorities try to keep secret, contains a haunted room where at least three occupants have sensed a presence, which evidently possesses a feminine air, as one person described it as a little girl, another believed it to be a young woman, while a third thought it was an elderly lady. Peter Tranchell, a fellow of Gonville and Caius College once visited a resident who was ill: leaving the bedroom he heard a rhythmic beating on wood. Returning upstairs, both he and the invalid accused each other of creating the sound.

ST. PETER'S TERRACE

St. Peter's Terrace is a row of large Victorian buildings running parallel with Trumpington Street, south of the Fitzwilliam Museum. One room is permanently locked, since from 1961 people have experienced strange and unpleasant sensations there, waking up at midnight with an overwhelming sense of evil. Although it was speculated that autosuggestion might have affected people's attitudes, and the chaplain of Peterhouse College said prayers in the room, a decision was eventually made to close it.

4 TRUMPINGTON STREET

The building at 4 Trumpington Street is divided between a restaurant and a language school. During the late Victorian period this was a private house called Cromwell Lodge. Mrs Jephson, the occupant, often heard footsteps on the stairs between 1 and 4am. Yet when she (or anybody who was in the house with her) looked, nothing could be seen. At other times footsteps ran around the top floor when it was known that nobody was there. A servant called Emma Ellis was going to bed at 10pm when she saw a girl wearing a hood standing by the door. The girl was very beautiful, yet Emma was so unnerved that she screamed and fainted. When she came around the hooded girl had vanished.

4 Trumpington Street.

The entities that haunted the building could be benign. Once Mrs. Jephson was worried about her son who was then in Scotland. She was awakened at midnight by the touch of a cold, clammy hand, to see 'a beautiful, ethereal figure with piercing oval eyes staring at her'. A few days later she received a letter from her son who was safe and well in Perth.

Between 1889 and 1892 Mrs Jephson took in a lodger, a University graduate called Mr. Joy, who often heard bells ringing between 1 and 2am. In 1895 Mr. Joy came back for a few days, bringing a friend called Mr. Hadath. They asked to stay in separate rooms, and, as a special show of bravery, Mr Hadath asked to stay in Mr. Joy's old room. That night they both heard rattling, like crockery shaking and breaking.

Each kept accusing the other of playing the fool until they heard the noises together. Then they heard 'bells of many varieties of tone and strength, it seemed as if every one in the house was ringing'. The cacophony woke Mrs. Jephson and her dog, who came into the hall. The bells stopped ringing and there was a brief silence, which was then broken by a loud repetitive clanging of metal being beaten. This was too much for the dog, who shot to the wall, cowering in terror. Joy and Hadath maintained a more rational appearance, but they, too, were terrified, and even after the noises stopped they were unable to sleep. Next morning both men left Cromwell Lodge, and never returned.

Perhaps the mystery of Cromwell Lodge was solved in 1899 when the house changed ownership and was being renovated. Three human skulls, two male and one female, were found under the dining room window. They were removed to the University Museum of Archaeology. No further activity has been reported in the building: the restaurant staff told the authors that they were unaware of any supernatural phenomena, or that the building had ever been thought to be haunted.

There is a strange feature of Mrs. Jephson's testimony. She saw 'a beautiful, ethereal figure with piercing oval eyes staring at her'. This sounds similar to figures reported in stories told by people who claim to have been abducted by UFOs. Sightings of UFOs were not as widely reported in the Victorian era as they have been since the Second World War (the expression flying saucer being created in 1947). Perhaps Mrs. Jephson saw an archetypal ghost figure who appearances were subject to other interpretations in an age before space travel was a scientific possibility.

THE MICHAELHOUSE CENTRE

In 2002 St. Michael's Church in Trinity Street was converted into The Michaelhouse Centre, a community resource building. Hemmed in by colleges, the church's congregation shrank so much that it was closed in 1908, after which it was practically abandoned. In 1963 two young men called Alan Attesley and Derek Cowling spent their weekends cleaning away the dust and debris from the interior. At about 11am one Saturday in summer, they entered by the south door, under the tower. Walking up the aisle, Alan saw a ball of light. About thirty inches in diameter, giving off a luminescent blue-white glow, it moved from the south door, through which they had just entered, travelling a little faster than walking speed. Derek then saw it. Both stood transfixed and Derek later said 'there was a chill which sent a shiver down the spine, and one's whole attention was held grippingly'. Perhaps psychic forces were stored in the church. Alan Attesley continued to live in Cambridge and confirmed his experience to Alan Murdie in 2001, but no paranormal incidents have been witnessed there recently.

TRINITY LANE

An ancient story of a prophetic apparition is associated with Trinity Lane, where an eleven year old boy saw a ghost in 1462, in front of Trinity Hall and Clare Colleges. On two days an old man with a long beard told the boy he would impart a message and then disappeared. On the third day he said:

> Go now and tell everybody that within these two years there will be such a pestilence and famine, and killing of men as no one living has seen before.

Members of the university wee impressed by this. The prediction may not have been wholly unexpected, as 'The Wars of the Roses' (as they came to be called) between different factions of the Plantagenet dynasty were then taking place, and would continue to flare up throughout the later part of the century.

THE ST. JOHN'S STREET POLTERGEIST

The street frontage of St John's College. The Victorian Divinity School, to the right, occupies the site of a house where poltergeist activity took place in 1694.

In 1694 poltergeist activity took place in a long demolished house in St. John's Street, occupied by Valentine Austin, a painter, and his wife. The house probably stood on the site of the Victorian Divinity School, opposite St. John's College. Over April and May noises were heard in and outside the house, and pebbles, stones, and even coins were thrown through the windows, breaking the glass. When the Reverend John Walker, vicar of the nearby church of the Holy Sepulchre (better known as 'The Round Church') brought several people into the house to pray (possibly planning to exorcise the entity) 'a great bellowing noise' was heard and a paint pot was hurled through the window, narrowly missing the vicar's head. Eventually four students of St. John's made a pact to enter with pistols and fire them at wherever the activity was coming from. When noises began to be heard next night they rushed into the house with loaded pistols, but the people there were (not unsurprisingly) alarmed at their arrival, and persuaded them not to shoot. Nevertheless, the shock may have cleared the environment, for the phenomena ceased.

THE BARON OF BEEF PUB

The Baron of Beef pub.

While tales of dead bodies or cremation ashes which are lost or remain unclaimed are a staple motif in 'urban myth' stories, an unclaimed cremation urn containing a dead person's ashes really did stand behind the bar of the Baron Of Beef pub in Bridge Street. When Bob Wass, the long serving landlord, died in the autumn of 2006, the Greene King brewery chain moved a relief manager named Damien into the pub. He told Alan Murdie that he had heard strange footsteps and a baby crying. Damien thought Bob Wass was haunting the pub, and was keen to be transferred again as soon as possible.

Soon after Vicky Evans took over the license. In December a wake was held in Bob Wass's honour, and in accordance with the tradition that the corpse be present, his ashes were placed on display. Bob's son asked if Vicky would look after the urn while he took his children to a party. Mr Wass junior never returned and has not been in contact since. Greene King breweries were unable to trace the Wass family, so Vicky put the ashes behind the bar where Alan Murdie often saw them. Shortly before Christmas Vicky and her mother heard an inexplicable moaning. One midnight in January Daisy, Vicky's old English sheepdog showed a strong reaction to something unseen in the bar. On 3 April 2007 Vicky's partner saw a fan behind the bar switch on by itself. Veteran Cambridge psychical researcher Tony Cornell said that The Baron Of Beef has had a long-standing reputation for low-level hauntings since the 1960's: there is a very unpleasant story that it was a brothel during the 18th century, when unwanted babies were born there and left abandoned upstairs.

The Baron Of Beef has since changed management: the ashes are no longer on display, and nobody on the staff is sure what happened to them. While it is uncertain if any activity has been noticed since, we would not be surprised if there are further reports.

FISHER LANE AND THE PICKEREL INN

Fisher Lane.

Fisher Lane is a narrow passageway running south from Magdalene Street, alongside the Pickerel Inn, near the bridge that gives Cambridge its name. In 1950 a former Cambridge student, who had completed his national service, married and rented rooms nearby. In the evenings he and his wife noticed a burning smell, unlike a cigarette, which they described as 'sweet', although they could find no fire. Enid Porter, the curator of the nearby Cambridge and County Folk Museum, observed that in the previous century lightermen who navigated barges along the Fen waterways lodged there. Like many Victorian Fen dwellers, they were not averse to smoking opium, then thought to have medicinal qualities and sold at King's Lynn docks. When conducting the Cambridge Ghost Walk Alan Murdie would pause to tell stories there. Six times between June 1998 and September 1999 participants noticed a smell like strong perfume or a sweet substance being burned; this was compared to opium. Alan himself smelt it at about 9.35 one windy Tuesday evening in July 1999. Other stories tell of a ghostly lady who runs down Fisher Lane, passing through the iron gates at the end to jump into the Cam. She may be the same ghost who haunts the adjacent Pickerel inn. Janis Spink, the

The Pickerel Inn. The entrance to Fisher Lane stands to the left (under the traffic sign).

manager, says this is haunted by a landlady who committed suicide by jumping into the Cam. Two landlords are said to have hanged themselves from the cellar hook in the public bar. If this is true the Pickerel must either have a very upsetting effect on those who work there, or attract exceptionally unhappy staff, but these may only be yarns told to frighten naïve pub-goers or entertain late night drinkers.

THE CAMBRIDGE AND COUNTY FOLK MUSEUM

The Cambridge and County Folk Museum.

The Cambridge and County Folk Museum opened in 1936 at 2 Castle Street, in the former White Horse Inn. The staff have been told that the ghost of a soldier in Civil War uniform can be seen at the top of the staircase where there was once a secret room. Parliamentary forces were based in Cambridge during the Civil War: although there is no clear evidence that they made use of the White Horse, it is not impossible that they could have been billeted there (or used its facilities when off-duty). None of the present museum staff has seen the phantom soldier,

The Museum staircase where a Civil War soldier was said to appear.

but unexplained footsteps were heard in the upper part of the building as recently as 1996. Enid Porter, curator from 1947 until 1976, was a brilliant folklorist who published a lifetime's research in *Cambridgeshire Customs And Folklore* (1969). Not only an outstanding and authoritative study of life and beliefs in the area, it is also a rattling good read which can be studied in detail, or simply skimmed through for numerous tales about local life, including some excellent ghost stories. Museum exhibits include charms, talismans and similar artefacts which were believed to bestow good or bad fortune on the owner or recipient, and objects made to protect people or buildings from witchcraft, evil spirits and ghosts. Perhaps the combined power of these exhibits has removed all ghosts from the museum!

THE ABBEY HOUSE

Paranormal phenomena have been observed at various locations around the wider limits of Cambridge. The Abbey House at the corner of Abbey Road and Beche Road, to the east of the city, deserves the title of 'the most haunted house in Cambridge'. It was built as a country mansion with stone from Barnwell Priory, which stood on the site before the Dissolution in 1539. By the nineteenth century Abbey House had come down in the world: as Cambridge expanded it was surrounded by Victorian terraces. It was divided into apartments, its gardens became overgrown and the walls began to crumble. Perhaps it was not surprising that it was widely believed that ghosts roamed the building and grounds.

The Abbey House.

A contemporary portrait of squire Jacob Butler of Abbey House.

Tradition says that Jacob Butler is a ghost whose spirit remains connected with the building. A towering, burly giant of a man, Jacob Butler stood six foot four inches tall. Educated as a lawyer at Christ's College between 1698 and 1703, he was often involved in legal disputes to reform corrupt practices in Cambridge. Inheriting the Abbey House in 1714 he re-built it, giving it its present appearance. When fairs came to Cambridge he held banquets for the giants, dwarfs and other performers. In his final years, when he took pride in being Britain's oldest barrister, he had his coffin made and placed it in the house's entrance hall, inviting visitors to sit in it and drink wine with him. His favourite companion at this time was a dog which he trained to walk on its hind legs. His unhappiness at his pet's death hastened his own death in 1765, aged 84. He was buried in the nearby churchyard of St. Andrew The Less, where he was commemorated by an elaborate memorial recounting his biography and genealogy.

John Lawson, a fellow of Pembroke College, (who would be awarded an OBE for his services to the Royal Navy in the First World War) lived in part of the Abbey House from 1903 to 1929, with his wife Dorothy and their four children (born between 1901 and 1906). On the night they arrived the Lawsons were frightened by a tremendous banging on a bedroom door. They thought their maid was playing tricks until she was found cowering under the bedclothes, more terrified than the children. Dorothy often felt somebody sitting with her and heard footsteps walking up and down the empty stairs. An intangible presence in an upstairs bedroom disturbed guests' sleep. John's brother, a heavy sleeper, stayed there and complained that he was woken up by something making 'an unholy noise'. Noises were heard from the room when it was empty. A servant heard faint voices, which she described as 'so pathetic', as well as clanking chains.

When the oldest two children were aged three and two they began to see a small furry brown creature running across the nursery on its hind legs: they called it 'Wolfie'. This might have been dismissed as childhood imagination until John and Dorothy saw it. John called it 'a nondescript kind of animal', which Dorothy identified as 'a furry thing of light sable colour moving tremendously quickly… I should say about two feet high'.

A phantom nun regularly came through John and Dorothy's bedroom, going to the foot of the bed, then passing to the curtains. The children regarded her as a guardian spirit watching them and the house. One night when it entered Dorothy thought compassion might release the spirit from its earthly confines, so she said: 'In the name of the Holy Trinity, poor soul, rest in peace'. The nun went to the curtain, appeared before John and a servant, then vanished. The Lawsons never saw her again, although she may not have left the house altogether, as Irish labourers who stayed there during the First World War would complain that she disturbed them.

Two weeks later a figure in a suit of armour briefly appeared before Dorothy. However, as time passed the Lawsons found that phenomena and appearances of ghosts became less frequent, and ceased during their final years in the house.

John and Dorothy kept secret records of their experiences, which were not published until 1972. Yet knowledge of the ghosts spread, and Arthur Beale's Gray's 1921 guidebook, *Cambridge Revisited*, mentioned that the Abbey House was haunted by a phantom animal which was seen by children rather than adults.

The Lawson's apartments were next occupied by Dr. Frank Coles Phillips of Corpus Christi College, who said he did not believe in ghosts. But guests staying in John and Dorothy's former bedroom heard footsteps and felt something moving around the room, and even across the bed. These followed the same pattern as those noted by the Lawsons, even though the furniture had been re-arranged. Then Dr. Philips saw the phantom animal run across an upstairs room on three successive nights. He left with his scepticism rather dented.

Harold Temperley, a master of Peterhouse College, who rented part of the house, knew four people who saw ghosts there. Later tenants included Celia Schofield, whose two year old son, Christopher, said he could see a 'tiny doggy' in the house. When a Raynor family moved in their teenage daughter, Ashling, heard whispering, and saw the nun in a mirror at the top of the stairs. In 1956 a couple called Miss Breaman and Miss Young stayed there: they had their dog, Raggy, put to sleep. Raggy would bounce a ball off a bed and jump after it. One night Mrs Raynor heard a ball being bounced on the floor, followed by the sound of a dog jumping. That night all the dogs in the area howled.

During 1999, when working for the University of Cambridge Local Examinations Syndicate, Robert Halliday met Phil Butler of Cambridge, whose grandparents lived in Abbey House in the 1920's. Several times Phil's grandmother saw a nun with a bunch of keys on a chain from her waist coming to the bottom of the staircase; as a teenager his father saw a little animal 'like a March Hare' running around.

In 1955 Professor Stratton, the University Professor of Astrophysics and the then president of the Society For Psychical Research, held a week long ghost watch in the house with Tony Cornell and the Cambridge University Society for Psychical Research. Participants concluded that people were most likely to experience phenomena soon after moving in. Possibly new arrivals disturb psychic forces, or people living in building become in some way acclimatised to them as time passes.

Conceivably Jacob Butler and his dog remained in some way drawn to the house after their deaths, while the figure resembling a nun either had some connection with Barnwell Priory which previously stood on the site. Alternatively, the apparitions may have had another origin, but people who saw them projected their ideas about the building's history onto them. It has been suggested that young children can sometimes be prone to see psychic phenomena which are not so readily observed by adults. This has certainly been the case at Abbey House, where several generations of children, who normally had no knowledge of the building's history, saw the phantom animal. The Lawson's children thought one ghost was a guardian spirit: perhaps he sensed that the presences were harmless, and may even have been taking a protective interest in the house and its occupants.

Archway made of stones from Barnwell Priory, in the grounds of Abbey House, adapted by the present residents with a statue of the Buddha.

The Windhorse Trust, a Buddhist charity, bought Abbey House as a hostel for modern Buddhists in 2002: they have renovated the building and tidied up the grounds. Robert Halliday asked the residents if they had any experiences. 'John' said he felt something sit on his bed and try to get into bed with him, but when he told it to go away it went. Other people say they have felt something pressing onto their chest, like a metal tray. One person saw semi-formed heads (probably male) floating in the haunted bedroom. 'Richard' heard that builders renovating the house twice saw a little animal running around. The Buddhists did not feel the presences as malevolent, and had no qualms about staying in the haunted rooms. They have since performed a Buddhist ceremony to move the spirits on, and hope this has released them to a further plane.

CUTTER FERRY PATH

TRINITY STREET.

Price 2d. Cambridge, Wednesday, January 25, 1928.

NEW CAMBRIDGE GHOST: UNCANNY VISITATIONS CAUSE COMMOTION.

"Hooded Monk," and "Bent Old Man": A Bold Spook!

Contemporary press report of the Cutter Ferry ghost from the 'Cambridge Chronicle': in the right hand picture a spectator points to a possible phantom.

Not far from the Abbey House, the Cutter Ferry carried people from Midsummer Common to Chesterton. In 1927 this was replaced by an iron footbridge, the Pye Bridge. On 17 December that year a ghost was seen in The Willows, a dank, marshy clump of woodland on the north of Cutter Ferry Path, between the modern Manhattan Drive and Elizabeth Way. It was seen again on New Year's Eve. It made further appearances in January 1928, and soon became a major topic of conversation across Cambridge. The Willows was partly flooded at the time, and the spot's damp, forlorn nature, combined with the nocturnal cries of a colony of owls in the trees, intensified the locations' eerie atmosphere.

One young woman was walking across Cutter Ferry Path on 20 January when she saw a luminous body three feet high bobbing up and down in the middle of the pool. She said:

> Although it was a pitch black night it was perfectly visible. It went to the bank and then returned to the water. I rubbed my eyes, but I was not mistaken, and by the time I reached the end of the lane I was running.

A young man saw the ghost hovering in a forty yard circle around an old tree stump. He was quoted as saying:

> It takes a wide course, then seems to come toward you with the speed of an express train, only to stop by the old stump. It always vanished into the same thick bush. At a distance it appears to be of a triangular shape, tapering towards the ground, and a little nearer there is distinctly to be seen the cowl of a hooded monk. Another time it was a good impression of a bent old man with a stick, varying from five to eight feet in height. It gives you a most wonderful feeling of fascination.

Some individuals who claimed to see the ghost said they had seen it drifting across the river from Abbey House. Up to fifty people might gather at The Willows at night, hoping to see it. A boy scout troop embarked on a spot of ghost hunting one evening, but the ghost failed to appear for them. One practical joker painted a face on a box and placed it on a tree branch with a sheet hanging from it, but this was quickly recognised. When another mischief maker turned up dressed in a sheet people pelted him with missiles. (This throws an interesting sidelight on some famous hauntings. It has been argued that some sightings are caused by auto-suggestion or manifested by practical jokers, but even the most naïve amateur ghost hunters have little difficulty in recognising trickery and treating it as such.)

Heavy rainfall at the end of January discouraged ghost hunters, and sightings ceased with the onset of spring. Since 1928 the area known as The Willows has since been drained. Although it is still open land there are fewer trees there, and no ghost has been spotted recently.

Misperception of natural phenomena can also occur, particularly in a state of heightened anticipation. Many people suggested that the mysterious lights and shapes were simply 'will o'the wisps' or 'Jack-O'-Lanterns', discharges of marsh gas, which have been common in the Cambridgeshire Fens. However, this theory has little foundation in chemistry. Other explanations include the possibility that anomalous weather created ball-lightning; or the phenomena were 'earthlights', electrical discharges created by friction between rocks below the earth's surface which have also been postulated to explain many UFO incidents. But the mysterious lights obviously made a great impression on all those who saw them.

25 MONTAGUE ROAD

A more conventional ghost (in the popular perception of these forms) was seen on a warm summer day in 1924 at 25 Montague Road. Geoffrey Wilson, aged ten, was playing in his grandparents' garden when he saw a young woman lying in a hammock in the summer house. He thought she was very attractive, if rather delicate and frail. Geoffrey paid her little attention. Returning to the house he described her. Everybody was startled, and told him that his description matched Stella Wilson, his father's younger sister. They were reticent to give further details, so it was only several years later that Geoffrey discovered that his aunt Stella had died of tuberculosis earlier that summer. She had tried to treat her condition by resting in a hammock in the summer house. He regarded this as an isolated incident in his life, for he had no great interest in the paranormal and never saw a ghost again. He said

> You could, I think, describe Stella's as a kindly ghost, as she made no effort to frighten a timid boy.

5 SELWYN GARDENS

Another ghost followed Margaret Verrall, a distinguished classics scholar, from Brighton to her Cambridge house at 5 Selwyn Gardens. One September evening in 1879, when she was twenty, Margaret was washing her hands in a room at the end of a passage leading to the front door of her family's Brighton home when she heard footsteps. Looking up she saw 'a little old lady' coming towards her wearing a long dark dress and a cap, with a grey knitted shawl over the shoulders fastened with a brooch. Although the figure was only a few feet away and clearly visible, Margaret could not distinguish any face. Neither startled nor alarmed, Margaret watched it approaching, when it vanished before her. Over the next few weeks she saw the figure at least three times, once when she was with her sister (who could not see it). Margaret's calm observation allowed her to note such details as the fact that the brooch fastening the shawl was like one worn by her great-grandmother, who had died ten years previously. The figure seemed life-like and fitted in with the surroundings, but the face remained 'a blank within the cap'.

5 Selwyn Gardens.

That autumn Margaret returned to Newnham College to resume her studies. She married Arthur Verrall, professor of classics at Trinity College. They moved into 5 Selwyn Gardens. Here the apparition re-appeared:

> One evening, as I was going upstairs to my room, I heard footsteps coming along the passage at the top of the house, and looking to the left (instead of turning to the right to my room) to see who it was, saw my old lady coming towards me. There was no-one else in the passage; the gas was lighted and I saw the figure plainly.

Margaret never saw it again. But this may have encouraged her to develop an interest in the supernatural, for she and her husband became keen students of the paranormal and close friends with leading members of the newly formed Society For Psychical Research, such as Frederic Myers, Edmund Gurney and Eleanor and Henry Sidgwick, colleagues at Trinity and Newnham, entertaining them at Selwyn Gardens (see pages 33-34). Frederic's death in 1901 caused Margaret to attempt mediumship, hoping to contact his spirit. She soon found that she excelled at automatic writing, a psychic skill where a medium produces written messages while holding a pen (or simply supporting it on the hand). Unlike many mediums Margaret did not need to enter a trance or fall asleep to produce messages, but only go into a light state of relaxation. Furthermore, the messages she produced were not short or banal like many mediumistic utterances but involved hundreds of cryptic and complicated passages in English, Latin, Greek and French, some of which seemed to predict future events. Her daughter Helen also took up automatic writing in 1903, marking the

Margaret Verrall.

start of a celebrated series of mediumistic communications known as 'The Cross-Correspondences'. When Margaret and Helen's communications were compared with those produced by other mediums in Britain and abroad, researchers noted certain similarities between the different scripts, suggesting that discarnate intelligences, possibly including Frederic Myers himself, were trying to communicate using a complex code. Scholars and researchers have analysed and debated the meaning of the Cross-Correspondences for over 100 years, regarding them as some of the strongest evidence for mediumship and survival after death.

ADDENBROOKE'S HOSPITAL

Not all ghosts haunt old buildings. Addenbrooke's Hospital opened in 1976 at the south end of Hills Road. An up-to-date, functional, modern medical facility, housing many scientifically trained staff, it is said to be haunted by a ghostly nurse, who killed herself out of guilt and remorse after mistakenly killing a patient to whom she gave the wrong dose of morphia. She re-appears when the drug is being administered again. Such tales are typical of the folklore that gathers in hospitals, or similar locations involving the transition between life and death. A more recent story appears in *The Motorcycle Hearse And Other Undertakings* (2006) the memoirs of the Rev. Ian Morris, a hospital chaplain (a conscientious member of hospital staff, who took his role in the medical profession very seriously, while keeping a sense of fun and humour).

A hospital porter told Ian Morris that lights and taps were being switched on, footsteps were being heard and bedpans were being moved in a certain ward (location withheld). Patients spoke of a nurse who visited them at night. Sensibly, Ian did not want to create panic, but looked for rational explanations, in case ordinary incidents were being misinterpreted or exaggerated. Staff were advised to observe events closely and keep written records of incidents. Even when the ward staff were on alert, no intruder or prankster was detected, but call buzzers sounded from an empty room, a television was switched on by itself and plugs were found pulled from sockets. Objects were found in unusual positions: paper cups were piled upright in the middle of the floor, and a box of tissues was found standing on top of a high traction frame. Ian and other staff tried to throw a similar box onto the traction frame, but found it impossible, as it would have had to have changed direction in mid-air. A missing Zimmer frame turned up behind a nurse's chair when she briefly left the ward. A nurse was asked to fetch a glass of water for a bedridden patient: on her return she discovered that an invisible presence had already supplied a full glass of water with a straw. A sheet was even changed under an immobile patient.

Agency staff who had no previous knowledge of the strange events saw phenomena. In the later stages furniture moved and doors opened by themselves. Once, at about 1 a.m., Ian saw milk pour from a drink machine, filling the drip tray. The milk was found to be unfit to drink, so the poltergeist had saved patients from drinking sour milk! He began to suspect that the poltergeist could be helpful.

Voices were heard, and finally two nurses heard a young woman's scream. Soon after the ward was closed for re-decoration. All staff and patients were transferred, and no unusual events were reported after it re-opened. Ian thought the ghost was

> A nurse who had loved her work and her patients and who had died suddenly – so suddenly that, bizarre as it may sound, she had not actually realised that her life's work had finished.

A year previously a nurse had worked on the ward, making her last shift before peacefully dying unexpectedly in her sleep. The mysterious scream was heard on the anniversary of her death.

RADIO CAMBRIDGESHIRE

The Hills Road headquarters of Radio Cambridgeshire, which opened in 1982, is also a modern, technologically sophisticated building, Yet studio 1 A has been a centre of activity since its opening. It is said to possess a strange atmosphere, and a distinct presence can be sensed there. Jacqueline Sheriff, a broadcast assistant, has heard 'a gravely voice' say 'hello' there. Ray Clark, an afternoon show presenter, first realised that the studio was haunted when he saw the misty outline of an old lady in a corner: after mentioning this he was told that other people had seen her, too. Sue Marchant arrived late for a broadcast one morning, when she saw a grey haired man, dressed in beige, sitting in the corner, who gave the message 'hey, calm down': she felt this allowed her to compose herself and deliver the programme without difficulty. Richard Spendlove, a local radio presenter, told Alan Murdie that racks of tapes have been inexplicably thrown across the room, and the studio can feel so sinister at night that some presenters refuse to broadcast from it, or even enter it. Thus the ghost seems ambivalent: frightening some people, but helping others: perhaps its activities are not necessarily intended to be unpleasant or frightening, but have just been interpreted that way by some of those who have encountered it. The Radio Cambridgeshire website has maintained a webcam link to Studio 1 A so people can watch for activity, and operate a ghostwatch from the comfort of their own home.

CAMBRIDGESHIRE GHOSTS

THE OLD VICARAGE, GRANTCHESTER

The Old Vicarage, Granchester, famous for its association with the poet Rupert Brooke, the focus of several paranormal events.

Some places within the Cambridge area are famous for ghosts, hauntings or paranormal activity. The Old Vicarage at Grantchester, on the southwest of Cambridge, has achieved immortality through the poet Rupert Brooke, who lodged there with the Neeve family. Described by W. B. Yeats as 'the handsomest young man in England', Rupert Brooke enlisted in the Navy in the First World War, when his early death in 1915, with the unfulfilled promise of youth cut short made him a romantic hero. One of his sonnets, *Hauntings*, is a poignant account of a ghost. In another evocative passage his eponymous poem about the Old Vicarage imagines the ghosts of famous Cambridge students meeting at *Byron's Pool*, the nearby beauty spot on the River Granta.

Dr A. I. Copeland was staying at the Old Vicarage in 1919, after demobilisation from the navy. One evening he and his bulldog, Caesar, heard 'slow, steady footsteps which came round the house and then up to the french windows' Caesar growled, and they jumped up to look outdoors. The moon was bright, but the garden was empty. Mr. Neeve told him:

> You have heard the ghost of the Old Vicarage. None of us has ever seen it. The footsteps come right up to the window. When we open it there is no-one there.

Dr. Copeland implied that Rupert Brooke was returning to the vicarage, but a lady called Enid Stuart Scott described an earlier apparition. On a hot summer day in 1911 her family were guests of the Neeve family. Everybody was in the garden when Enid saw a young man and a young woman in old-fashioned costume, arms entwined, the girl's head resting on the man's shoulder, exuding an aura of love and happiness. They were walking directly towards Enid's parents, yet both couples appeared oblivious to each other. Enid was about to call a warning when something stopped her. The couple then vanished and Enid realised that only she had seen them. She kept her experience secret until after her marriage, when she told her mother. Only after that did she find that the Old Vicarage was haunted.

In 2007 Kathy Skin of Cambridge recalled a previously unpublished episode for Robert Halliday. In 1936 or 1937 Kathy and her mother went to a fete in the Vicarage grounds. They were sitting at a bench with two strangers, before a cut yew hedge, when a lady and a little girl came along the path from behind them. The lady was very tall, carrying a parasol, wearing a cream coloured bustle with a ground-length dress; the girl wore a poke bonnet, a three-quarter length skirt and button-up boots (old-fashioned costumes even then). Talking animatedly, they walked through a gap in the hedge, although Kathy and her fellow fete-goers never heard what they said. The four fete-goers met again later that day in the gardens and had tea together, observing that they had not seen the oddly-dressed couple again, and wondering if they were going to a fancy-dress event. Neither Kathy nor her mother saw the other two fete-goers again. Next year they went to another event at the Old Vicarage. They found the place where they sat previously, but there was no trace of the yew hedge. Seeing an old gardener they asked about the hedge: he said he had cut it down many years ago. Like Enid Stuart Scott, did they see a past event being re-enacted?

A 'folly' in the Vicarage garden is called 'the ruin'. Peter Ward, an owner of the Old Vicarage, who ran for Britain in the 1936 Olympics, operated a printing works there. In the 1950's Peter told a story that he and a colleague often found printing letters in strange patterns. They suspected each other of playing tricks until one day when snow fell. They left 'the ruin' making footprints in the snow. Next morning they found the letters in patterns, but there were no other footprints. Peter Ward was quoted as saying:

> Our home is pretty full of manifestations of all kinds, all of them pleasant and harmless, none of them appears to be connected in any way with Rupert Brooke but with earlier happenings in the house... Having lived with them for fifty years I now take our ghosts for granted and live very much at peace with them.

MADINGLEY HALL

In *The Old Vicarage Grantchester* Rupert Brooke wrote

> And things are done you'd not believe
> At Madingley on Christmas Eve.

Perhaps this implied that paranormal activity took place at Madingley Hall, for there are stories of ghosts appearing here. Madingley Hall, six miles west of Cambridge, was built in 1543 by Sir John Hinde, who dismantled St. Etheldreda's church at Histon for building material. In the seventeenth century the heiress of the Hindes married Sir John Cotton: their descendants lived there until Victorian times. The Hall is now the headquarters of the Cambridge University Board of Extramural Studies. Thomas Harding, an Edwardian owner of the Hall wrote *Tales Of Madingley* (1912), a romantic novel about the building's history, which told how Sir John Hinde's mother, Lady Ursula, was devoutly religious. Upset that her family demolished a church to build the Hall, her discontented spirit haunted the building. It is unclear if the story of Lady Ursula's ghost pre-dated Thomas Harding's arrival at the Hall, or if he invented it for his novel, on the assumption that no Tudor mansion would be complete without at least one resident ghost!

Madingley Hall.

A stout lady in black is said to walk from the Park Gates to the Hall at Christmas, while a young woman dressed in white like a bride walks along 'the cloisters' to the north. Little is known about the dark lady, but the white lady is said to be mourning for her love: either because he was killed, or because she was not allowed to marry him: sometimes she is called 'Jane', although nobody knows if she is a Hinde or Cotton.

The gardens are the setting for an intriguing timeslip. Late one September afternoon a woman (who requested anonymity) took her poodle for a walk around the gardens on the north side of the Hall. As they went round a large circular path she heard voices, but nobody was there. The dog's tail dropped between its legs and it became frightened. Turning around she saw a young man hanging in an awkward position over the stone balustrade, his arms dangling in a peculiar way. He wore a ruff around his neck, his hair was cut dark and jagged, and his face was greenish white, like a skeleton, expressing a hate that made her shiver. She could think of nothing else to do but to walk on. When she returned the garden was empty. She wondered if it was imagination, until one day when she went back and encountered the same thing. She mentioned this to a gardener, and he said he had undergone a similar experience.

In 1980 Frances Ison, a local woman, described some occurrences at the Hall. An Irish lady, whom she called 'Molly', cycled to Madingley, and was exploring the grounds when she suddenly felt very cold, and thought she was being watched. Turning around, Molly saw three men in cavalier style clothing standing in the flower garden staring at her. Their expressions were so 'awesome' that Molly ran to her bicycle and peddled home as fast as she could: when she arrived home she was trembling and icy cold. Molly spent two weeks in bed with shock, and never visited Madingley Hall again. It is tempting to speculate that these appearances of cavalier figures who give upsetting looks are connected.

SAWSTON HALL

The ghosts of Sawston Hall, six miles south of Cambridge, are well-known. Sawston Hall is often cited as one of the haunted stately homes of England. It is said that Queen Mary Tudor's ghost walks in the dress that she wears in her portrait there. Contrary to popular tradition, which regards her as an angry, embittered person, her ghost is supposed to smile and exude happiness. Mary was a Roman Catholic: when Protestants tried to prevent her succession to the throne in 1553 she sheltered with the Huddleston family at Sawston (who had also remained loyal to the Roman Catholic faith). After she left Protestant pursuers burned their house: Mary said she would give the Huddlestons a finer one, and allowed them to take stone from Cambridge Castle to build the present Hall, where they lived until 1970.

Sawston Hall.

Unfortunately it is uncertain if there are any witness accounts of Mary's ghost, or if the Hall's reputation as a haunted building pre-dates the mid-twentieth century. The first resident to publicly report paranormal activity was Clare, who married Captain Reginald Eyre-Huddleston in 1930. She heard a spinet (a keyboard instrument popular in Tudor times) playing there. Her friends heard it too, although Reginald did not. Clare obviously had a sensitive musical ear: there was a harpsichord in the Hall, but she said the tone was lighter, and that she heard it when she knew the harpsichord was not being played.

In 1960 Mrs. Fuller, the cook, said she had seen a silent ghost drifting in and out of one room, while the British Travel and Holidays Association sponsored Candy Scott, a model, to sleep in the Tapestry Room (said to be the most haunted room). Candy saw nothing, but felt icy winds and heard noises including doors opening and closing, which convinced her that the hall was haunted. In 1984 *Cambridge Evening News* reporter Carmel Fitzsimons stayed at Sawston Hall for a Halloween feature: although she saw no ghosts, she slept badly and caught flu.

When the authors visited Sawston Hall in about 2000 they thought the tree lined drive from Church Lane to the Hall felt rather oppressive and claustrophobic. Although unable to gain access to the Hall, they explored the outside, and noticed that the Hall and grounds were surrounded with thick trees which they felt gave it a spooky appearance.

Bruce Milner of the Sawston Village History Society informed Robert Halliday that he participated in a ghost watch in the Hall during September 2004 (when the building was unoccupied and nearly empty of furniture). Although nobody actually saw a ghost, one woman was quite insistent that she felt a little girl holding her hand in the Long Gallery, while a 'medium' experienced a feeling of a person falling down stairs and breaking his neck. Some people also felt strong 'vibrations' suggesting a presence at other places in the Hall, including the cellar.

In 1999 Philip ('Phil') Butler of Cambridge told Robert Halliday a previously unknown story about Sawston Hall. In 1996 Phil's son became friendly with the son of a lessee of the Hall, who ran a language school there. The two of them were in the domestic quarters, and one of them hung his jacket over a sofa. Suddenly the atmosphere became very cold.

Then the jacket stood up on the sofa, as if somebody was wearing it, and stood suspended in the air for at least a minute. The temperature then returned to normal and the jacket flopped back down onto the sofa, when it felt warm, as if somebody had just taken it off.

THE CLOTHES TEARING POLTERGEIST OF SAWSTON

The Tanner's House in Sawston High Street.

In 1804 the Tanner's House, a Queen Anne building at 149 High Street, Sawston, was the setting for a remarkable poltergeist that tore clothes. At that time an Adams family lived there. In October 1804 Mrs. Adams kept finding tears in her dress: after five days she put on a new one, but rips began to appear in this, too. Within a week six of Mrs. Adams's dresses had been damaged, always while she was wearing them. Then Mr. Adams's clothes and the maid's dresses began to be slashed. A fifteen-year-old niece staying with the family 'had only the body part of her gown remaining, the skirts having dropped off as she moved about'. The torn clothes were exhibited in Cambridge; Isaac Milner, the master of Queen's College (one of the leading scientists of the time) and John Torkington, the Vice-Chancellor of the University were asked for opinions, although it is not known if they reached any conclusion. The Huddleston family of Sawston Hall observed that the clothes were well-made, yet so ragged 'that no beggar would accept them'. Many people visited the Tanner's House, yet, even if they kept a watch on their clothes, these would still be torn. One young woman visiting them found her dress ripped in four places while she was there, which so frightened her that she ran from the house nearly fainting. The case featured in *The Morning Chronicle*, where an anonymous Sawston poet wrote:

> This miracle is surely wrought
> By wizards or by witches,
> Unseen, unfelt it rends the coat,
> But never hurts the britches.

The Times published the (rather implausible) suggestion that it was caused by the discharge of underground gases, reporting

> The mystery of the fiery spirit whose pranks have excited so much wonder at Cambridge, remains still unsolved; and will, probably, become the subject of a new play or novel for the delight and terror of the spectre loving circles.

While tearing of fabric has accompanied some cases of poltergeist activity, situations in which it has been confined to tearing clothes are unusual, to say the least: as *The Times* surmised, its potential development in the hands of some ghost story writers would be quite remarkable. Like many poltergeist cases, it ceased after a few days. The presence of an adolescent girl may have been the trigger: *The Cambridge Chronicle* implies that the niece was thought to be responsible, but many clothes were torn while people were wearing them, and if she was simply tearing clothes from sheer wilfulness, it seems strange that she was not detected, and one of Mrs. Adams's dresses was torn four times while she was at a friend's house. (Activity took place in a house owned by an Adams family: it seems an amusing co-incidence, although it is just that, that there was a 1960's television 'situation comedy', since revived in several films, about *The Addams Family*, who had the personas of horror-film characters.)

THE OLD FERRY BOAT INN, HOLYWELL

One well-known story, which appears in numerous books, to a point where it has been cited as one of the classic English ghost stories, is told about the Old Ferry Boat Inn at Holywell, neat St. Ives, seventeen miles northwest of Cambridge. 'Juliet Tewsley' materialises here on the anniversary of her death, 17 March 1050 (which happens to be St. Patrick's Day), points at her grave, a flagstone in the bar floor, and dematerialises into the ground. She is the tragic shade of a young woman who fell in love with a local woodcutter named Thomas Zoul: he did not return her love, and she hanged herself in despair. Suicides were then buried at crossroads, so she was buried at the junction of a track to the ferry and the River Ouse. A large flat stone was placed over her grave. Centuries later the inn was built over the spot.

The Old ferry Boat Inn at Holywell.

The story is often quoted as an ancient legend. In fact, it only originated with an investigation carried out in 1953 by the Cambridge University Society for Psychical Research (C.U.S.P.R.), led by Tony Cornell. On 17 March 2003, the investigation's fiftieth anniversary was marked by an event organised by the Ghost Club, with Tony Cornell, then in his eighties, as guest of honour. Tony Cornell described how the C.U.S.P.R. was asked to investigate a vague local tradition that a ghost walked in The Ferry Boat on 17 March. This had never previously appeared in print, and nobody is now certain how the Society heard the story or why they decided to investigate. They held séances with a Ouija Board when they received messages, purporting to come from an entity called Juliet Tewsley, who told the sad story of her death in 1050. Tony Cornell admits the details do not add up: the name Juliet was invented by Shakespeare, 500 years after the ghost's alleged earthly existence, and no corroborative evidence of Juliet Tewsley or Thomas Zoul's existence has ever been found. (Furthermore most séances were held in The Blue Boar in Cambridge's Trinity Street.)

An investigation was scheduled to be held in the Ferry Boat on 17 March 1953, when the landlord promised C.U.S.P.R. members a free meal. The news had leaked out, and the inn was invaded by an army of press reporters, accompanied by hordes of sightseers, filling the pub to overflowing, with crowds of spectators watching through the windows. While the pub did a roaring trade, psychic research was impossible, and the C.U.S.P.R. never even received their promised meal! Press reporters approached the vicar of Holywell, who initially rubbished everything as nonsense, but within a few days was re-telling Juliet Tewsley's story in detail, adding new information of his own!

Subsequent investigations in 1954 and 1955 were thwarted by further hoards of reporters, revellers and sightseers, who were coming to regard 17 March as an opportunity for drinking and merriment. By then Juliet Tewsley had impressed herself on public imagination. Local folk musicians performing at the 2003 event recited a poem about Juliet Tewsley which they claimed had circulated since the eighteenth century!

Occasional phenomena have been reported at the Ferry Boat (although nothing quite as breathtaking as an apparition over the reputed grave). Since the 1960's cleaning staff have heard footsteps crossing the bar. Some time before 1973 visitors arriving by boat one 16 March asked the landlord if manifestations might take place. He replied 'She'll not make herself known tonight' whereupon a tankard was lifted from its hook and thrown across the bar. A Peterborough couple who arrived separately at the 2003 event said they had visited the pub on 17 March 1993 and seen a strange light in the windows. Their 1993 visit was purely co-incidental, and they did not know the inn was said to be haunted until they told the staff and regulars of their experience. They were therefore making a return trip, hoping for a repeat. (Two other visitors from Dublin came via Cornwall, having initially confused the two English towns called St. Ives.) Altogether the fiftieth anniversary re-investigation provided a most memorable evening and there is no doubt that the story of Juliet's Tewsley's ghost has become a show that will run and run.

CAXTON GIBBET

Caxton Gibbet must be one of the most obviously macabre spots in the area: the sinister and ominous structure of a gibbet by the highway would send a shiver down many spines! Twelve miles west of Cambridge, at the crossroads of the A428 and the A1198, leading to St. Neots, Huntingdon and Royston, it is one of England's best known gibbets, although it has been replaced several times, the present structure being made in 1934 with wood from a demolished timer-framed building. After the First World War a dummy representing the Kaiser was hung on the gibbet, and an effigy of Arthur Scargill was suspended here during the 1984-5 miners' strike.

In 1753 John Gatward of Royston, waylaid John Pink, a postboy and stole the mailbags. He was hanged, and his body gibbeted here. William Cole, the rector of Milton, near Cambridge, wrote:

> I saw him (Gatward) hanging, in a scarlet coat, and after he had hung about two or three months it is supposed that the screw was filed which supported him, and that he fell in the first high wind after. Mr. Lord of Trinity (College) passed by as he lay on the ground, and, trying to open his breast to see what state the body was in, not being offensive, but quite dry, a button of brass came off, which he preserves to this day.

It seems incredible that the gibbeting of corpses was sufficiently common for a clergyman to write about it with detachment, while a senior member of Cambridge University could rifle the body with equanimity.

Sketch of Caxton Gibbet in 1902.

There is a folktale that a man murdered the members of a family called Partridge in the adjoining parish of Bourn and fled abroad. Seven years later he returned, unrecognised. Going to a pub he had too much to drink and boasted that he had once destroyed a nest of partridges. A quick-witted local realised the truth behind this jest and alerted the authorities. The murderer was brought to justice and hanged alive on Caxton Gibbet to die a lingering death. A passing baker who took pity on him and gave him a loaf of bread was hanged beside him. (Although variants of this story appear across England, in the last few centuries murderers have not been suspended alive and left to die: only the dead body was gibbeted.) However, there may be some factual basis in this tale, as Bourn parish registers say that Richard Forster, his wife and child were murdered in 1671.

'A Gibbet': print by Thomas Rowlandson (1756-1827).

A nearby coaching inn, The George, was popularly called The Caxton Gibbet. Legend said that a landlord stole guests' belongings while they slept. Once three guests shared a room: when the landlord was rifling their luggage one woke: the landlord murdered the guest, then killed the other two before they could wake to raise the alarm, and hid the bodies in the well. The bodies were found and the landlord was hanged and gibbeted next to his inn. The room where the murders took place was always intensely cold. The original inn burnt down in the 1920's, and was replaced by a modern pub. This became a Chinese restaurant, which was also devastated by fire on 21 March 2009: it is uncertain whether the ruins will be rebuilt or demolished.

CARLTON RECTORY

The authors have encountered a story of a haunting at Carlton Rectory, fifteen miles southeast of Cambridge. Told in about 1933 by John Saltmarsh, a Fellow of King's College, Cambridge, in a lecture to the defunct Eastern Counties Folklore Society, it can be found in the society's archives in Cambridge University Library. We found it so compelling that we have decided to reprint it verbatim.

> The trouble all began with the rebuilding of the rectory, or, according to tradition, much further back. In the eighteenth century it was said there was a disgraceful parson at Carlton who would sit up all night drinking with his butler. One evening, over their cups, the two fell out; and the butler killed the parson or the parson the butler: I cannot now recollect. The difference is not material, for the other was promptly hanged and there seems to be no doubt that it was the parson's ghost which afterwards haunted the rectory. What trouble he gave his successors I do not know. But in the seventies or eighties of the last century [i.e. 1870-90] a young clergyman moved in with a young and impressionable wife and found it necessary to take drastic action. He therefore, and remember that I am relating this not as fact, but as local tradition, he therefore secured the assistance of eleven other parsons, and the twelve of them held a service over the ghost and forced it into a bottle, which they swiftly corked and quickly sealed. They then locked it in a cupboard in the rector's study, threw the key into the horse pond, and had the cupboard papered over, so that in the course of time everyone forgot that a cupboard was there.
>
> The rector lived a long life and his incumbency ended some fourteen years ago. Then, as I say, the rectory was partly pulled down, and partly rebuilt; and that little jobbing

> builder who carried out the work found the cupboard and found the bottle, and pulled the cork to see what was inside. He reported that a little thin vapour came out of the bottle, and what was left behind appeared to be beer. And then all the trouble began: footsteps in the dead of night, doors opening and shutting; once, it is said, a face with a pointed beard was seen peering out from behind some curtains. Nor was the trouble confined to the rectory; there were footsteps in the village that people feared to pass along, because of the rectory ghost. The end of the story is rather tame; the ghost continued to give trouble for some weeks; but as far as I am aware, no fresh exorcism was needed; he seems at length to have quietly faded away, without the assistance of bell, book or candle. Let me repeat it once more, I do not recount these incidents as being the truth; but as what was commonly reported to be happening to our neighbours at the time.

A variant of this tale appears in Justin Brooke's *Suffolk Prospect* (1963), about rural life just over the county boundary in Wickhambrook. Justin knew a builder who was asked to do some work in the Rectory. When the housekeeper warned him that a ghost had been sealed in a bottle in a cupboard he decided to play a practical joke: he found an old bottle and opened it in front of the housekeeper. She turned pale and fled the room. The Rector was upset and angry, saying such stories should not be treated as mere superstition as they could contain some truth.

Carlton Rectory was originally a moated manor house: part of the moat remains, as a garden pond. In 1832 the rector, William Boldero, returned home from visiting another clergyman, went into the garden and failed to return. The servants found he had drowned in the pond: why or how remains a mystery. The tragedy impressed itself on local folklore: the memory of William Boldero's mysterious death almost certainly influenced the story of the Rectory ghost.

The former Rectory at Carlton.

Carlton is a small village and has long ceased to have a resident clergyman: the Rectory is now a private house where the Wylie family run a kennels for dogs. In 1999 Robert Halliday spoke to Robin Wylie, who had lived there since he was two years old: he knew of a legend that a butler killed a rector before drowning himself in the pond, but was unaware of the stories that Robert Halliday had located. Robin felt tranquillity there: he thought the Reverend Boldero's spirit felt glad he was taking good care of the house. While he only sensed things, his daughter Polly had seen a man in an upstairs bedroom, standing by a corner fireplace with a cupboard above it, (which sounds similar to the place where the ghost had been locked). Polly's music centre used to turn itself on, and, earlier that year the daily help had come down and asked why the mirror should have been in the middle of the room. In 2010 Polly told *Fortean Times* that she felt the presence was friendly.

THE GHOSTS OF BABRAHAM

Babraham Church.

Babraham Church, seven miles southwest of Cambridge, contains an amazing seventeenth century baroque monument displaying life-sized standing statues of Richard and Thomas Bennett of Babraham Hall. Their ghosts are said to walk in the nearby fields, and appear in Eveline Barnard's *The Brothers Are Walking* (1976) a novel set in the Babraham area. A local joke says the brothers' spirits can no longer rest, as the Jones family, who owned the Hall after the Bennetts, removed the Bennett's coffins from the family vault to make way for themselves. The grounds of Babraham Hall join the churchyard: there are stories (although few specific details are available) that it is haunted by an unseen lady whose skirts can be heard swishing along a corridor. Once a boy aged only thirty months old said he saw a lady go through a wall.

THE GOGMAGOG HILLS

A tour of regional ghosts comes a full circle with The Gogmagog Hills, four miles southwest of Cambridge. The highest point in the county, they rise to 234 feet (71 metres) above sea level, and are topped by an iron age hillfort called Wandlebury. Archaeological excavation suggests that this was dug between the third century BC and the start of the Christian era. In the eighteenth century the Godolphin family built a house in the hillfort and imparked the hilltop. Gog and Magog appear in the books of Ezekiel and Revelation in the Bible as fearsome giants: medieval legend identified them as the last survivors of a race of giants who once lived in Britain. Wandlebury means 'Waendel's burgh' (or enclosure). Waendel was a figure in dark age mythology, whom the Anglo-Saxons often associated with great prehistoric monuments. Now run by the Cambridge Preservation Society as a country park and nature reserve, 'The Gogs' are a pleasant place in which to enjoy the delights of the countryside.

The ramparts at Wandlebury on the Gogmagog Hills.

Over the seventeenth and eighteenth centuries there are mentions of hill figures cut in chalk on the Gogmagog Hills. The archaeologist T. C. Lethbridge tried to find and re-excavate these in 1955 by probing the ground with a steel rod. His fellow archaeologists denounced his findings: rejection of his work was one reason why he abandoned archaeology for paranormal research (see also pages 34-5). Subsequent investigations have found no evidence of soil disturbance in the area where Lethbridge worked. (The figures probably lay inside Wandlebury, and would therefore have been destroyed when the Godolphins imparked the hillfort.) The cleared section of Lethbridge's hill figures has been allowed to grass over. Although they cannot be regarded as monuments of antiquity, they form an unconventional curiosity, and their loss would be regrettable.

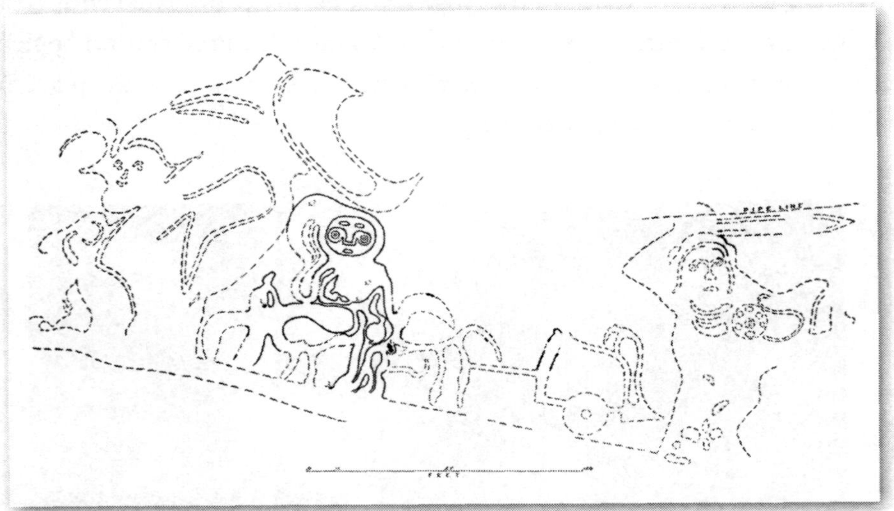

Outline of hillfigures which T.C. Lethbridge plotted on the South slope of the Gogmagog Hills in 1955. Only the central figure, represented by continuous lines, was excavated.

The Wandlebury Rings are the setting for a spectacular tale of a knight and a phantom horse, recorded by Gervase of Tilbury. Born in the twelfth century, Gervase travelled Europe as a scholar and diplomat before writing his *Otia Imperalia* (*Tales For An Emperor)* in 1211, a collection of 'wonder tales' about fantastic happenings and events.

Gervase wrote that if a knight enters Wandlebury at dead of night when the moon is shining, and calls 'knight to knight come forth' another knight appears on horseback and charges: one of the two will be overthrown. The challenger must enter the rings alone although other people can watch from outside. A knight called Osbert Fitzhugh was staying in Cambridge when he heard the story, he rode to Wandlebury and called 'knight to knight come forth!' The phantom warrior appeared and charged, but Osbert unhorsed it on their first clash. Osbert decided to take the horse: as he did so the phantom threw a lance, wounding his thigh. Returning to Cambridge he was acclaimed a hero, but at cockcrow the horse broke free and was never seen again. Every year, Osbert's wound bled on the anniversary of the contest.

A knight called Osbert Fitzhugh founded a monastery at Westwood in Worcestershire. Romantic tales that merged fact and fantasy were popular in the twelfth and thirteenth centuries (this was when the Arthurian legends were being devised). The Wandlebury legend includes two standard motifs from a story of an encounter with an other-worldly realm: the hero acquires a valuable possession which is lost or snatched away, and is left with an inexplicable scar or wound as a reminder of his adventure.

The authors have encountered an oral tradition that the fast running footsteps of an invisible horse are sometimes said to be heard around the Gogmagog Hills: could this be the phantom horse described by Gervase of Tilbury?

Bill Clark, who was warden of the Gogmagog Hills for 26 years, is an excellent raconteur of stories about the location and his time there. He told one man about the phantom horse. The man sceptically dismissed the story, but he later came running back to Bill in terror, saying he had seen a horse rush by with jingling harness.

Bill tells another story, which has entered local folklore. One bright sunny day in 1975 he was taking a party of schoolchildren around the area when a twelve year old girl began to scream. She said a man in funny clothes had walked around a bush and stood staring at her. The supervising teacher said the girl was truthful, sensible and not imaginative. On a later school trip to the Fitzwilliam Museum she pointed out a model of a Roman solider as looking like the man who frightened her.

Two years later a woman saw the soldier, although her husband who was with her saw nothing. In about 1980 Bill's wife, Wendy, was with a family visiting the hills. Wendy and the three children saw a man walk from behind a tree: he was grey all over, including his clothes, and wearing a grey helmet, but the parents saw nothing.

In 1985 Bill Clark was supervising some foresters who were cutting down a large and unsafe beech tree. One of Bill's tasks was to warn anybody approaching to keep well clear. As the tree was about to fall, Bill saw a man in a grey anorak standing under the line of descent. Terrified for the man's peril (and callous stupidity) Bill charged towards him at top speed, yelling at him to watch out, and planning to drag him to safety. As Bill reached the spot where the man stood there was nobody there. Just then the beech tree crashed down, the outer branches missing Bill by a mere six inches. The tree-fellers were amazed at Bill's behaviour: as the tree began to topple, they saw Bill, whom they knew to be an experienced nature warden, run straight towards it. They had not seen the grey man at any time. Evidently the ghost of the Gogmagog Hills could only be observed by select people at certain times. Possibly the impact of the falling tree laid it to rest, as it has not been seen since.

It is a telling detail that the Gogmagog Hills were the setting for the tale of a spectral knight on horseback in the middle ages, resulting in the first ever ghost hunt in Cambridge. Modern visitors, some of whom know nothing of the site's history, have also had paranormal encounters with a ghost in armour and a phantom horse: over 800 years a phantom warrior has guarded this area of Cambridge: who can tell how the paranormal will manifest itself over the next millennium?

BIBLIOGRAPHY & REFERENCES

The essential starting point for anybody wishing to research any aspect of Cambridge should be *The Cambridgeshire Collection*, the local studies department of Cambridge Central Library, in Lion Yard, Cambridge. This is an inexhaustible mine of information on the long and fascinating history of the city and university of Cambridge and the county of Cambridgeshire, with a very helpful and knowledgeable staff: many of the published sources quoted below can be found here.

As one of the United Kingdom legal deposit libraries, Cambridge University Library holds a large collection of books and reference materials which also proved useful in many ways. Most importantly for the production of this book, it holds the archives of the Society for Psychical Research, with numerous unpublished case studies of ghosts and hauntings. The archives of the long defunct Eastern Counties Folklore Society, also placed here, are another useful source of information for those wishing to study Cambridgeshire beliefs and traditions.

The authors have made use of the parish registers of Bourn and St. Benedict's (or Benet's) church in Cambridge: these, like most such records from Cambridgeshire, are now stored in the County Record Office in Shire Hall on Castle Hill, Cambridge; microfiche copies can also be consulted in *The Cambridgeshire Collection* (see above).

The British Library in London provided a further unique source of information: the archives of the Ghost Club between 1882 and 1936.

CAMBRIDGE COLLEGE GHOSTS

KING'S COLLEGE

M. R. James regarded the writing of ghost stories as a hobby, and a diversion from a busy and demanding career as a university administrator, college tutor and academic researcher. His output was rather less than one story a year during his adult life. During his lifetime he published four collections in book form: *Ghost Stories Of An Antiquary* (1904); *More Ghost Stories Of An Antiquary* (1911); *A Thin Ghost And Others* (1919) and *A Warning To The Curious* (1925), a total of twenty five stories. These and five other tales appeared in M. R. James, *Collected Ghost Stories* (1931), which have been frequently reprinted and anthologised. *Casting The Runes And Other Ghost Stories* (edited by Michael Cox, 1987), includes eighteen of these, and a further three written after 1931, annotated with explanatory notes, combined with a selection of M. R. James's personal observations on supernatural fiction and a critical introduction. M. R. James also wrote a supernatural novella for children, *The Five Jars* (1922) which seldom appears in anthologies of his work and remains surprisingly rare.

M. R. James's autobiography, *Eton And Kings* (1929), mentions the Gibbs Building ghost, but tells little about his interest in the paranormal. For an introduction to his life, work, and the milieu in which he operated, Michael Cox: *M. R. James, An Informal Portrait* (1983), is an up-to-date and readable biography.

Jacqueline Simpson, 'the rules of folklore in the ghost stories of M. R. James' *Folklore* 108 (1997) 9-18 investigates how he used and developed folklore in his stories.

Beryl Dyson, *Great Livermere: A Parish With Ghosts* (1981), a privately published pamphlet, describes fourteen ghosts seen in M. R. James's home village in Suffolk: some details are abstracted in Alan Murdie, 'Ghostwatch', *Fortean Times* 220 (March 2007) 20-1.

A Pleasing Terror: The Complete Supernatural Writings Of M. R. James (2001) was issued in a limited edition of 1,000 copies by the Ash Tree Press of Ashcroft, British Columbia, Canada, (which specialises in classic ghost stories). This contains all of M. R. James's known stories, including several unfinished tales he deemed unfit for publication, along with his academic writings on ghosts, combined with critical and academic studies of his stories and their influence on the genre of supernatural fiction, and a list of radio, television and stage adaptations of his stories. Unfortunately a copy may cost between £250 and £400.

Ghosts And Scholars edited by Richard Dalby and Rosemary Pardoe (1987) contains a selection of ghost stories in the Jamesian tradition, some set in Cambridge. Rosemary Pardoe has instituted the *Ghosts And Scholars M. R. James Newsletter* and the *Ghosts And Scholars* website, dedicated to M. R. James and other antiquarian ghost story writers: http://www.users.globalnet.co.uk/~pardos/GS.html.

CORPUS CHRISTI COLLEGE

Cambridge University Library, Department of Manuscripts, Archives of the Society for Psychical Research, case file H.70.

The parish registers of St. Benedict's (St. Benet's) Church, Cambridgeshire County Record Office.

'A college ghost' *The Occult Review* March 1905, 129-33. (Written anonymously, but containing clues that identify the author as Llewellyn Powys.)

C. Pollock, 'The story of the Corpus ghost', *Corpus Association Newsletter* 39 (1960) 14-15.

C. H. E. Smith 'The Corpus ghost', *Corpus Association Newsletter* 45 (1966) 40-44.

Arthur Beales Gray, *Cambridge Revisited* (1921).

John Venn, *Alumni Cantabrigienses: A Biographical List of All Known Students, Graduates and Holders of Office At The University of Cambridge, From The Earliest Times To 1900.* Part I: *From The Earliest Times To 1751* (4 vols., 1922-1927).

Shane Leslie, *The Cantab* (1926) and *The Film Of Memory* (1938).

Patrick Bury, *The College of Corpus Christi, A History From 1822 to 1952* (1952).

Peter Martland and Miles Pattenden *Corpus Lives, 1352-2002* (2003).

Graham Chainey, *A Literary History Of Cambridge* (1985).

'Table Talk column', *Cambridge Daily News* 24 December 1904.

The Corpus Christi College website, http://www.corpus.cam.ac.uk.

CLARE COLLEGE

Owen Seaman, *Paulopostprandials, Only Some Little Stories After Hall* (1883).

M. D. Forbes, *History Of Clare College 1326-1926* (two vols., 1930).

Cambridge Daily News 26 September 1930.

SIDNEY SUSSEX COLLEGE

Karl Pearson and G. M. Morant, *The Portraiture Of Oliver Cromwell With Specific Reference To The Wilkinson Head* (1935).

C. Parish, The posthumous history of Oliver Cromwell's head', in D. E. D. Beales and H. B. Nisbet, *Sidney Sussex College, Historical Essays In Commemoration Of The Quatercentenary*, (1996) 105-10.

Nicholas Rogers and Christopher Parish, *Cromwell And Sidney Sussex* (pamphlet published by the college, 1999).

W. Kent, 'Cromwell's head', *East Anglian Magazine* September 1946, 10-13 and 49.

G. L. Horn, 'The head of Oliver Cromwell', *East Anglian Magazine*, December 1954, 108-9.

Cambridge Advertiser 11-18 August 1841.

Cambridge Chronicle 14 August 1841.

The Times 12 August 1841.

Varsity 18 November 1967.

Untitled account of activity, *Sidney Sussex College Annual* (1989) 35.

TRINITY COLLEGE

This might be the place to lay one ghost story to rest. Robert Halliday has encountered a story that a fellow of Trinity appeared in the college chapel after his death. This seems to derive from a humorous article, 'phantom phellows' *Varsity* 11 November 1994, a tongue-in-cheek feature on University hauntings, which included the author's story of how he was greatly amused by a passage in a book that told how 'a fellow continued to attend services in Trinity College for some time after his death'. He cited this as an example of how a badly worded passage can be misunderstood, but this seems to have been misinterpreted by some as describing an actual haunting.

Archives of the Ghost Club, British Library, Department of Western Manuscripts, Additional Manuscripts 52258-52273.

Notes And Queries first series 9 (18 February 1854) 150-1.

William Howitt, *History Of The Supernatural* (1863).

Life And Letters Of Fenton John Anthony Hort By His Son A. F. Hort (1896).

Life And Letters Of Brooke Foss Westcott By His Son A. Westcott (1903).

Alan Gauld, *The Founders Of Psychical Research* (1968).

Renee Haynes, *The Society For Psychical Research 1882-1982, A History* (1982).

The story of the ghost in a hunting outfit appears in T. C. Lethbridge's first specialist study of the paranormal, *Ghost And Ghoul* (1962). He wrote six further books on parapsychology (sprinkled with anecdotes from his archaeological career); his widow, Mina Lethbridge, produced a seventh, posthumous, book from his manuscripts. A summary of his theories appears in Tom Graves, *The Essential T. C. Lethbridge* (1982). Although the authors do not necessarily support all Lethbridge's theories, they regard some of his ideas in this field as being worthy of consideration. *The Sons Of T. C. Lethbridge* is a website dedicated to Lethbridge studies: http://www.tc-lethbridge.com

Terry Welbourn, a member of *The Sons Of T. C. Lethbridge* is engaged on a biography of Lethbridge, but no publication date has been scheduled.

The Ghost Club and the Society For Psychical Research maintain websites: http://www.ghostclub.org.uk and http://www.spr.ac.uk.

JESUS COLLEGE

Archives of the Ghost Club, British Library, Department of Western Manuscripts, Additional Manuscripts 52258-52273.

Arthur Gray, *Brief Tedious Tales Of Granta And Gramarye* was first published in 1919; the Oleander Press of Cambridge produced a facsimile paperback edition in 2009.

Enid Porter, *Cambridgeshire Customs And Folklore* (1969).

Arthur Gray's obituary, *The Times* 15 April 1940.

Cambridge Evening News 18 October and 31 November 1977.

Arthur Gray's *A History Of Jesus College, Cambridge* (1902) provides a full history of the institution until the end of the nineteenth century (although it does not include any ghost stories). A second edition, revised by Frederick Brittain (1979) continues the college's history until the mid-twentieth century, outlining Arthur Gray's mastership, and mentioning the *Everlasting Club*. Further information about Arthur Gray can be found on the *Ghosts And Scholars* website, http://www.users.globalnet.co.uk/~pardos/GS.html.

CHRIST'S COLLEGE

Arthur Ponsford Baker, *A College Mystery* (1918), (facsimile edition produced by *Back-In-Print Books*, 2004).

Michael Wyatt, '*A College Mystery* - a further mystery?' *Christ's College Magazine* 223 (1998) 38.

Rosemary Pardoe 'A.P. Baker and *A College Mystery*' *The Ghosts And Scholars M. R. James Newsletter* 8 (2005) 11-15.

'The dead among us', *Newsletter, The Magazine Of The Staff Of The University Of Cambridge* November-December 2009, 8-10.

'Cambridge - a paranormal history' *Varsity* 30 March 2010.

ST JOHN'S COLLEGE

R. F. Scott (editor), *Admissions To The College Of St. John The Evangelist In The University Of Cambridge*. Part III, July 1715 - November 1767 (1903); Part IV, July 1767 - July 1802 (1931).

Enid Porter, *Cambridgeshire Customs And Folklore* (1969).

Cambridge Independent Press 1 January 1960.

Peter Linehan, 'Unfinished business', *The Eagle* 2001, 32-9.

EMMANUEL COLLEGE

Cambridge University Library, Department of Manuscripts, Society for Psychical Research, case file H.69.

ST CATHERINE'S COLLEGE

'College notes', *St. Catherine's Society Magazine*, 1931, 16.

'College newsletter', *St. Catherine's Society Magazine*, 1965, 57.

'Memoirs of Mr S. J. Alderton', *St. Catherine's Society Magazine*, 1980, 24.

A. D. Cornell, *Investigating The Paranormal* (2002).

PETERHOUSE COLLEGE

'Obituary', *Gentleman's Magazine* October 1789, 957.

'Biographical anecdotes', *Gentleman's Magazine* November 1789, 1049.

Philip Pattenden, 'What the butler saw: high spirits in college', *Peterhouse Annual Record* 1997-8, 66-72.

Cambridge Evening News 19 December 1997.

Daily Telegraph 19 December 1997.

The Times 19 December 1997.

The Times Higher Education Supplement 19 December 1997; 2 January 1998.

The Independent 20 December 1997.

D. A. Winstanley, *Unreformed Cambridge* (1935).

CITY CENTRE GHOSTS

RAINBOW VEGETARIAN RESTAURANT

Sarah ('Sadie') Barnett's obituary appeared in *The Daily Telegraph* 15 August 1991, and is reprinted in Georgia Powell and Katherine Ramsey, *Chin Up Girls, A Book Of Women's Obituaries From The Daily Telegraph* (2005).

THE HAUNTED BOOKSHOP

Cambridge Weekly News 20 August 1987.

The Cambridge Insider 22 January - 4 February 1988.

Podcast interview with Sarah Key by Cambridge Time Traveller on 3 November 2009, http://timetraveller.209radio.co.uk.

THE OLD BOROUGH LIBRARY

Cambridge Daily News 4 October 1968

THE PHANTOM PICTURE

Thomas Thornely, 'The lady of Trumpington Street', *The Cam* February 1937, 62.

Enid Porter, *Cambridgeshire Customs And Folklore* (1969).

SILVER STREET

Alan Gauld, 'A Cambridge Apparition', *Journal of the Society For Psychical Research* 38 (1955) 89-91.

ST PETER'S TERRACE

Varsity, 4 February 1961.

Cambridge Time Traveller website, http://www.cambridgetimetraveller.com.

LITTLE ST MARY'S LANE

Cambridge Evening News 7 April 1971.

4 TRUMPINGTON STREET

Cambridge University Library, Department of Manuscripts, Society for Psychical Research, case file G.266.

Untitled paper, *Journal Of The Society For Psychical Research* 10 (1901) 43-7.

THE MICHAELHOUSE CENTRE

Cambridge University Library, Department of Manuscripts, Society for Psychical Research, case file H.474.

TRINITY LANE

'Brief Notes Of Occurrences Under Henry VI and Edward IV' in *Three Fifteenth Century Chronicles*, edited by James Gairdner, Camden Society, second series, 28 (1880).

ST JOHN'S STREET

The Diary Of Abraham De La Pryme, Surtees Society Publications, 54 (1870).

FISHER LANE

Enid Porter, *Cambridgeshire Customs And Folklore* (1969).

Cambridge Independent Press 1 January 1960.

Cambridge Evening News, 27 August 1998.

THE FOLK MUSEUM

Arthur Beales Gray, *Cambridge Revisited* (1921).

Enid Porter, *Cambridgeshire Customs And Folklore* (1969).

'Enid Porter (1909-1984)', in Hilda Ellis Davidson and Carmen Blacker, *Women and Tradition, A Neglected Group of Folklorists* (2000), 231-44.

GHOSTS IN THE CAMBRIDGE SUBURBS

THE ABBEY HOUSE

Cambridge University Library, Department of Manuscripts, Society for Psychical Research, case file H.157.

Alan Gauld, 'The haunting of Abbey House, Cambridge', *Journal of the Society For Psychical Research* 40 (1972) 109-23.

Arthur Beales Gray, *Cambridge Revisited* (1921).

Enid Porter, *Cambridgeshire Customs And Folklore* (1969).

Cambridge Independent Press 1 January 1960.

Cambridge Evening News 22 December 1972.

For Jacob Butler see an anonymous pamphlet *The History Of Barnwell Abbey Near Cambridge With The Origin Of Stourbridge Fair* (1806) and Charles Henry Cooper, *Annals Of Cambridge* (five vols., 1842-1908, re-published in paperback by Cambridge University Press, 2009).

CUTTER FERRY PATH

Cambridge Chronicle 25 January 1928.

Cambridge Independent Press 27 January 1928.

Cambridge Daily News 30 January 1928.

MONTAGUE ROAD

Dennis Bardens, *Ghosts And Hauntings* (1965).

SELWYN GARDENS

'Report on the census of hallucinations', *Proceedings Of The Society For Psychical Research* 10 (1894) 120-22.

'On a series of automatic writings by Mrs. A. W. Verrall', *Proceedings Of The Society For Psychical Research* 20 (1906) 1-433.

'Mrs. A. W. Verrall: obituary notice', *Proceedings Of The Society For Psychical Research* 29 (1916) 170-6.

ADDENBROOKE'S HOSPITAL

Anthony Hippisley Coxe, *Haunted Britain* (1973).

Ian Morris, *The Motorcycle Hearse And Other Undertakings: Stories From The Life And Work Of A Hospital Chaplain* (2006).

Cambridge Time Traveller website, http://www.cambridgetimetraveller.com.

RADIO CAMBRIDGESHIRE

The BBC Radio Cambridgeshire website,
http://news.bbc.co.uk/local/cambridgeshire/hi/tv_and_radio.

CAMBRIDGESHIRE GHOSTS

THE OLD VICARAGE, GRANTCHESTER

Enid Stuart Scot, 'The Ghosts Of Grantchester', *Evergreen*, Summer 1986, 50-53.

The Marchioness Townshend and Maude Ffoulkes, *True Ghost Stories* (1936).

Roy Christian, *Ghosts And Legends* (1972).

Peter Scarisbrick, 'Memories of the Old Vicarage' *The Rupert Brooke Society Journal*, Spring 2006, 27-29.

MADINGLEY HALL

Cambridge University Library, Department of Manuscripts, Society For Psychical Research, case file H 157 A.

Frances Ison, *Madingley Reminiscences* (1980) typescript in the Cambridgeshire Collection, F12.0904 .

T. W. Harding, *Tales Of Madingley* (1912).

Dennis Bardens *Ghosts And Hauntings* (1965).

Cambridge Evening News 24 December 1980.

SAWSTON HALL

Cambridge University Library, Department of Manuscripts, Society for Psychical Research, case file H.419.

Diana Norman, *The Stately Ghosts Of England* (1963).

Dennis Bardens, *Ghosts And Hauntings* (1965).

John Harries, *The Ghost Hunter's Road Book* (1968).

Peter Underwood, *Gazetteer Of British Ghosts* (1971).

Andrew Green, *Our Haunted Kingdom* (1973).

Joan Forman, *Haunted East Anglia* (1974).

Cambridge Daily News 6 January 1960.

Sunday Telegraph Weekend Magazine 28 October 1966.

Cambridge Evening News 31 October 1984.

THE CLOTHES TEARING POLTERGEIST OF SAWSTON

The Morning Chronicle 9 and 13 October 1804.

Cambridge Chronicle 13 October 1804.

The Times 15 October 1804.

Traviss Teversham, *The Huddleston Documents Of Sawston Hall* (1970).

THE FERRY BOAT INN, HOLYWELL

Anthony Donald ('Tony') Cornell gave the full story of his investigations at Holywell in *Investigating The Paranormal* (2002). (reprinting transcripts of the séances from Cambridge University Library, Department of Manuscripts, Society for Psychical Research, case file H.406). Books that quote the story of Juliet Tewsley as a historical episode (or as a long-established legend) include John Harries, *The Ghost Hunter's Road Book* (1968); Peter Underwood, *Gazetteer Of British Ghosts* (1971) ; Anthony Hippisley-Cox, *Haunted Britain* (1973); Marc Alexander, *Haunted Inns* (1973); Guy Lyon Playfair, *The Haunted Pub Guide* (1985); John Brooks *Britain's Haunted Heritage* (1990) and Richard Jones, *Haunted Britain And Ireland* (2002). Joan Forman, *Haunted East Anglia* (1974) contains an impartial discussion of haunting based on press cuttings she saw on display in the Ferryboat, which show that it need not have been too difficult for any conscientious researcher to establish that the story is a recent invention.

CAXTON GIBBET

Cambridge University Library, Department of Manuscripts, Society for Psychical Research, case file H.414.

The parish registers of Bourn Church, Cambridgeshire County Record Office.

David Mossop, *Caxton Gibbet*, typescript in the Cambridgeshire Collection, R.06.2904.

Charles G. Harper, *The Cambridge Ely and King's Lynn Road* (1902).

William Mortlock Palmer, *Notes On Cambridgeshire Villages*, no 2, *Caxton* (1927).

Enid Porter, *Cambridgeshire Customs And Folklore* (1969).

The Cambridge Express 10 June 1893.

Cambridge Evening News 2 November 1950; 30 March 1989; 6 October 1989.

The Peterborough Citizen 7 December 1973.

Albert Hartshorne, *Hanging In Chains* (1891, reprinted in paperback, 2008) is the only specialist study of the practice of gibbeting criminals.

CARLTON RECTORY

Archives of the Eastern Counties Folklore Society, Cambridge University Library, Department of Manuscripts, Additional Manuscripts 7515.

'Obituary', *Gentleman's Magazine* May 1832, 474.

Justin Brooke, *Suffolk Prospect* (1963).

Alan Murdie, 'Ghostwatch', *Fortean Times* 262 (May 2010) 14-15.

BABRAHAM

Eveline Barnard, *The Brothers Are Walking* (1976).

The village website, http://babraham-village.net.

THE GOGMAGOG HILLS

Gervase of Tilbury's *Otia Imperialia (Recreation For An Emperor)* edited and translated by S. E. Banks and J. W. Binns (Oxford Medieval Texts, 2002).

T. C. Lethbridge, *Gog Magog: The Buried Gods* (1957).

Arthur Gray, 'On the Wandlebury legend', *Proceedings Of The Cambridge Antiquarian Society* 15 (1910) 53-62.

Jacqueline Simpson, 'Waendel and the Long Man Of Wilmington', *Folklore* 90 (1970) 25-8.

Gladys Goetinck, 'The Wandlebury Legend and Welsh Romance', *Proceedings Of The Cambridge Antiquarian Society* 71 (1988) 105-8.

Wendy Clark, *Once Around Wandlebury* (1985).

Cambridge Time Traveller website, http://www.cambridgetimetraveller.com.

Lightning Source UK Ltd.
Milton Keynes UK
12 October 2010

161164UK00001B/50/P